CW00351281

A
CHANGE
OF MIND

SOCIOLOGICAL INSIGHTS
INTO MENTAL DISORDERS

by
Mark Evans

DORRANCE PUBLISHING CO., INC.
PITTSBURGH, PENNSYLVANIA 15222

Copyright © 1994 by Mark Evans
All rights reserved
ISBN # 0-8059-3473-1
Printed in the United States of America

First Printing

Dedication

*To all those good, brave people who helped to trans-
form state psychiatric hospitals into more humane
places, and in doing so, reversed a nightmare.*

Contents

Chapter 1

Something Wrong Upstairs

"I mean I can understand someone needing the occasional early night, but it's every single night now—nine o'clock crashed out in bed. I ask her why, she says she's tired. We used to go out a lot, but not now. She says she can't face it. 'Face what?' I ask her."

"Oh, I don't know," she says. "I guess I'm just tired?"

"It doesn't seem normal to me, somehow it seems, well—abnormal. But maybe I'm wrong; who am I to judge my own wife? But there's something wrong somewhere."

* * * * *

"I can't quite put my finger on it, but he's definitely been moving away from us. Just twelve months ago his life was so full—sports, studies, girlfriends, and us. We used to see so much of him, confident and sure of himself. But now, well...he goes out most of the day just aimlessly walking around town, often on his own, usually in the middle of winter without a coat. A friend of mine suggested the other day that I discuss it all with a doctor, a psychiatrist she meant, but I won't bother. Probably it's just a teenage phase, yet it doesn't seem right at all; it's making me unhappy.

"And I'm watching him fall apart, not bothering to shave, change his clothes, hardly speaking to a soul all day. In winter when the central heating is on, he goes round opening all the windows. I asked him why and he told me not to bother him, quiz him, check up on him, or inquire into every little thing he does or says. One day he said that he wondered if I was any longer his mother, that I'd turned into a detective. He says I spy on him sometimes and follow him round, but the truth is I don't, never. Perhaps he's just going through a bad patch, but it's been going on for over two years. If I saw a doctor about it, they might put him in one of those loony bins, and I'd never want to do that to my own flesh and blood. But he's so strange at times, difficult to talk to, be with, live with, and it hurts."

* * * * *

Such tragic juxtapositions of ourselves coupled with incomprehension find themselves not in specialized, hived-off institutions of our contemporary mental health complex; instead they are a lot closer to home. In fact, the setting is invariably just that—the home, somewhere in a street, in a sprawling city. That is the physical setting. No whitewashed walls, reeking of bleach, people marching impersonally in white coats down long corridors. For such a scene is the very last lap—confinement. The last lap of what may have been a hell of a race to have had to run—much sweat lost, many tears shed. In a way, contrary to popular opinion, it is the institution which is the most congenial stage. Beds ready made, wards spic and span, drugs immediately accessible in cabinets, televisions to watch. Admittedly very artificial but at least something, whereas the city streets yield nothing. Thus the institution is the icing on the cake. This is the fear of the end of the line—the loony bin, funny farm, cracker factory; call it what you will, the rest home. It's gardens, fountains, warbling birds basking in sunshine. This kaleidoscopic riot of colour constitutes the heaven, the sanctuary. So that fear is misplaced or, more accurately, the tragedy is. The real struggle is out there in society—the iceberg beneath water level. The institution is merely the tip. For the bitter frustrations concealed in ostensibly peaceful bedrooms, boardrooms, factories, and shops are the genesis of the tragedy. We tend to look right past the every day essence of the problem in its manifestations of harrowed faces that walk past us, wrongly imagining the problem is entirely contained in the white home on a remote forsaken hill; in the asylum. We desperately desire to avoid contact or even contemplate that somewhere in our midst is insanity. After all, who wants to even suspect or desire to assume that one's own husband is *going a bit weird*? Which loving wife seriously wishes to even remotely have an inkling of such a horrifying possibility? Far easier then to immediately dismiss, reject such

2

a happening as totally impossible. And yet in the end, after landing up in a hospital, this amazingly complex and flexible love is still as strong.

"I'll definitely be up to visit, as soon as I can, I love you."

"You won't be there long. They know what they're doing, those people looking after you. Everything's going to be alright."

"Any problems with money, just let me know. I'll also send a parcel, write every day. I miss you so bad, but it won't be for long in there. Keep fingers crossed."

Although it is only in a minority of cases that relatives acquiesce to their own kin's removal from home to hospital, there is very often the heavily built-in expectation that the stay will be pleasant and short. Unfortunately, this is by no means always the case. This is so for a number of reasons. There may be no progress in the patient's mental state, even a regression, and whether or not this is true or untrue is *not* the decision of either patient or relatives. It is mainly up to the respective consultant, for doctors have a virtual monopoly in such areas, regardless of however anybody else sees things. But for practical reasons this is almost inevitable, not through lack of manpower, but "mindpower." Supposedly, few people are qualified to diagnose and make undisputed opinions on psychiatric patients. This is the sphere of the doctor, the responsible medical officer, or R.M.O. for short. Yet to just consider patients and family in this non-legal way can be very narrowly misleading. There is, side-by-side, the far larger enterprise (daily expanding) or forensic psychiatry. Here discharge dates, time spent away, are highly clouded in a vagueness which is impenetrable, not just by the patient but even to the consultant. For this reflects the really amorphous nature of mental disorder, complicated by legal transgression, bringing into the scene parties such as medics, media, nursing staff, and police. It is often a confusing, unspecific, with much buck passing overshadowed by many misperceptions and misunderstandings.

So far the picture presented is that of patients, families, and institutions in a rather over-neat, objective way, heavily biased towards a clinical, deterministic model. We have had a detached scientific perspective instead of subjectively trying to interpret our topic as a product of a wider, growing malaise endemic to modern social life. Also, the above introductory paragraphs captured a snapshot after the illness had taken root. We here will be attempting to go a step back and try and find its antecedent patterns or causation. But this is not to revamp ad nauseam the old, well worn *victims of society* clause. Neither will the polarizational extremes of *born mad* or *learned by the environment* receive much scrutiny. We shall look instead *within* the ends of the continuum to dynamic sets of predispositional effects. But still, a lot can be learned from older debates and work, which can usefully be inserted into the themes to be followed.

Of course, it would be a lot easier not to listen to any of the above debates and just forget mental ill health. Simply to continue to believe in the myth of a sane, normal existence impeccably clothed in a fictitiously stable self-righteousness. But, to use that well worn but eternally relevant cliche—what about *the thin line*? How close is our non-existent, stereotypical law abiding citizen to a dubiously wobbly status as regards deviance? Or even to go the whole hog—to a state of clinical derangement? Let us look at a few typical people, the word "typical" meaning it could easily be anybody, or any sex, country, or point in time. Those chosen have a location in society of a somewhat marginalised status but, as will be seen, they possess not strikingly obvious disadvantage concerning their own faculties, they are not born to fail or come unstuck. Instead, their victimization stems from a set of societal influences of an all-pervasive nature which can strike at random, though is often insidiously cumulative. The actual impact is indiscriminate, impersonal, and unpredictable. The characters selected are not rare specimens in glass cases in some modern museum, possessing unusual attributes of pathological affliction. We are not privileged in a capacity of superiority to stand cooly at a distance and point at such characters and on the way out breath out, saying "Phew! Thank God that's not me," for the whole point is that such a blissful utterance of relief once passed through their lips as perhaps it may yet pass through ours. If you had told them that a mental demise would one day be their fate they would have laughed in your face, they simply couldn't have contemplated it, let alone prevented it. In other words those we see or more often hear about—the mad—could one day be you or me. Nobody has any special passport of immunity to avoid crossing *the thin line*.

Joe Bloggs is a human being; he's never been in any serious legal trouble and he's never received psychiatric treatment. He has been more or less content with his life so far because he is still only in his early twenties. He has no financial problems and he manages to get plenty of girls. Yet recently he's found himself getting sick to death of the same routine of answering about three telephones at once, being stuck behind the same desk, same workmates, same tea-breaks, and even his social life has acquired an air of monotony.

It's been noticed by his boss that some spark in Joe seems to have disappeared, his interests are waning and with it that "get up and go" feature that everyone, until recently, so much identified with Joe and admired. The worst thing of all is that Joe is himself aware of it, but somehow cannot quite pin down the whole problem's origins or understand it in its entirety. He cannot easily *relate* to anybody about it. Joe can understand the drudgery of his office job—paperwork, day in day out, but a change of job for similar remuneration is definitely out of the question because Joe doesn't possess a wide flexibility of skills. This is sometimes referred to as a job crisis, but is a much wider crisis of rupturing of relationships associated with the job's demise. Joe decided, after tentative advice from his boss, to have a chat about his difficulties with "someone who knows about this sort of thing." So Joe does. Three days later he's on an average dosage of tranquillisers— pills to help him relax, if not totally cope—but still he cannot for the very life of him break out of an increasingly oppressive sense of disillusionment. The doctor he sees says it is a cause for genuine concern, that Joe is suffering from a neurotic condition. The advice is to spend a short stay in a local psychiatric unit. To this Joe, somewhat confused, uncertainly consents— the idea being for a rest, a break, "to get away from it all." The outlook is less favourable for the future—perhaps on pills for several years and connections, if not permanent residence, in the hospital.

Joe never works again full time, just drifting from job to job, which seem to be dead end, short lived, and poorly paid. Accompanying this downward spiral are a loss of dignity, self-respect, and self-confidence, along with a sharp reduction of social contacts. Joe Bloggs is a psychiatric patient. Later we shall have good reason to answer the question of why many of Joe's office colleagues (in similar positions to Joe occupationally and socially) did not fall by the wayside; that is, didn't succumb to pressure and crack. You might immediately say, "Well, Joe just couldn't cope, whereas others manage to, that's all!" But it's not *just* Joe, is it? It was not a condition contained in the head of one person on earth...millions today are Joe Bloggs, and it is occurring at an increasing rate, too. So, at this juncture we can say that it might be one of two explanations. The more obvious and less credible one is that millions of people lack social coping skills. The other and more deep one is that people in modern society suffer breakdowns because they can see through social, political, and economic facades which they hither to have had to robotically fit into, adjust to, put up with, and pay up service to. It may be perceptive disillusionment, an individually insightful undermining of current social life which precipitated their sense of no longer possessing roots, any anchorage to a system they have grown both sad and cynical of.

Unfortunately for Joe, there is no easy escape from such an undesirable reality, no readily forthcoming alternatives or substitutes. In other words, a little philosophy or insight by Joe in his office in the big, impersonal city has led him to reject a lot of what surrounded him, circumscribed him, so he failed in the conventional context and importantly *defined* in a derogatory way—not as perceptive or cynic but perhaps depressive or neurotic. There again the answer may not be so simple as reasoned above, for there are many disagreements as to exactly what constitutes insanity. We also can ponder as to whether or not normality is a specific state of mind fixed unalterably for all time or instead something quite different. It could be that there is no biological or natural essence remotely connected with normality but rather, historically, quite specific conventions which have to legally fit in with historically specific (but changeable over time) sets of conventional wisdom. Another way of saying this is that each era, epoch, chunk of social life in time, in space has its own very particular normality. And standards appropriate to one normal era may be inappropriate, even frowned upon as deviant, in another.

What is proper and improper conduct are not absolute things but fleeting, flexible, humanly constructed entities. This can be seen with the homosexual or the lesbian. What may well be biologically inherited can be socially skewed to appear opprobrious in some social settings and periods to markedly different degrees. Shifting moralities affect legal attitudes and have real effects on our evaluations of ourselves and others for all legal codes are humanly constructed. Homosexuality in England was, for instance, a crime forty years ago. Such views emanating from this affected, quite seriously, many peoples' livelihoods. Such shifting perspectives, that is the historical plasticity of evaluations, will be a key current running throughout discussions, especially the fact that what is labelled as and unthinkingly passes as "it's only natural," or "it's unnatural" is, in fact, nothing of the sort. For there is very little that is *natural* about human beings. Instead, there are almost infinite norms, values which conflict between different groups in society, all struggling for mastery of the most widely acceptable (at the time) ideology which best services their interests. Attempts to change a set of ideas—denaturalize and hence demystify them strip them of myth, expose them as the umbrella of a dominant group's self interests—causes a countervailing, often forceful reaction from the threatened group. Often this air of *naturalness*, which certain groups claim is the very fabric of their set of ideas, standards, and morality, is called factual. It is said to be a system of undisputed *facts*, but facts are not tangible things; instead only standards given a legitimating stamp. Facts do not speak; they have to be interpreted, can be easily disputed. *Facts* have no sacrosanct objective yardstick for all time. Instead, *facts* are humanly selective interests often given an undeserved claim to be an objectively, tangible, natural essence. Joe Bloggs was indeed beginning to think along such lines.

Similarly, of dubious plausibility are claims to the *truth. Truths* are not divine or laid-down external, disembodied things laid down for all time by some supreme mind. They are simply the successful laid-down personal views of a person or group at some point in human history and location in society. The successful or unsuccessful nature of a truthful thing is directly dependent on its believability—how many people accept it and adhere to it and for how long they persist in this. Connected to true or untrue statements are patterns of domination; the currently dominant group's power depends upon a perpetuation (which such a group will engineer) of belief by those who are the dominant groups' subjects—the dominated. So that ultimately there are perhaps no fixed *truths*, only patterns of power supported by sets of ideas passing under the heading of *truth*. That is, what is today labelled and claimed to be *true* is an idea, nothing more than that, and given the many competing groups in human society, all are competing for ascendancy. There are many equally valid competing *truths*; that is, rival ideologies by rival groups in a non-consensual society.

The above digression may appear to have been something of a diversion but is not necessarily an irrelevance. Such themes do not lead up cul de sacs; rather they shed light on a problem pleading for illumination. The theory is needed to help us get out of straight jackets of many long-believed, taken-for-granted *facts* and supposed *truths*. In order to break new ground, it is imperative we examine in a critical, even sceptical light, our hitherto received, dearly held assumptions. Admittedly this can be very difficult, as all our sensory imputed knowledge has possessed a *naturalness* about it. We can relate such an argument to the two social statuses touched upon above—the sexually *deviant*, as categorised by society. If such people are continually being told that their behaviour is abnormal or even that their identities are disgusting, they often tend to come to believe this; it is a self-fulfilling prophecy. They may succumb to, even absorb to, the stigma which is vented upon them to the point which it makes them lonely, isolated (they feel far from *normal*) and even to contract a serious nervous disorder. They go underground, undercover, hiding from what is professed as a *healthy* sexual majority in society. Such devaluations of self-esteem take their toll, leading to a socially demoralized state in which admission voluntarily to a mental hospital may occur, as much as a refuge as a "cure" for their "afflictions." We can see here a pressurized situation of changing peoples' identities if they are not regarded as *normal* or *towing the line*. Transformations cannot just stop at sane to insane, but responsible to institutionalized—depending upon the time spent inside an institution. Often it can be waving good-bye to all you knew and all you had, all you ever wanted. The usurpation of your very individuality is suffocated under the anonymous blanket of your hospital bed.

So much for theory. Let us now turn to our final case study. As always a lot of people are only aware in hindsight; that is, after the event and its often harmful consequences. Epitomizing this par excellence was the dream-cum-nightmare of the high rise flat, or tower block. "Very costly," "inefficient," "not really aesthetic." Such terms euphemistically hide the gore spread out after someone hopelessly at wit's end plunged from a balcony high above. Perhaps if it hadn't been that particular scenario it might have been a different location, such as a mental hospital. But the victim either didn't know about it anyway, or didn't know who to contact for help. Yet doubtless—the result may well have been just the same—no hope with which to fuel a continuation of meaningful life. So that the young, single parent mother of three children was "sick and tired" of lifts that wouldn't operate properly, or wrecked by vandalism, or just simply the fact that being 150 feet off the ground was a breakage of a link, a severing of what she had always known. As she looked out of the window, not at people, shops, cars, or trees, but just and only at the sky, without stretching the metaphor too much, she may have even realized there was no heaven, just a reality she no longer belonged to. Simply an impersonal, inhuman sky. Other hardships—insufficient income, ill physical health, utter loneliness, and a start of mental turmoil—may all have unbearably accumulated and coincided before walking out onto that balcony. Was it mental illness per se to lead to it? Was she depressed? Most important of all, was it her *fault*? All three questions can be cogently answered in the negative. For the most part people don't ask to be unhappy, they don't request loneliness and depression, and very few request a horrible death. Arguably, her life of former variety, pleasure, hope, and other people was truncated by an extremely ill thought-out form of accommodation. Once again hindsight and only hindsight eases the explanation. Nonetheless, surely tower block construction at its infancy, even pilot stage, should have been realized by its planners as a totally unacceptable inhuman project to say the very least. So that if the unfortunate woman was presented with a hell in which to spend her days, why should she have been prepared to endure it? Human beings are amazingly resilient, but not super-beings. It is true we can only take so much. This can also be summed up by saying that people are always affected by and affect other people whenever there are differences of self-interests and power.

Further arguments will amplify such themes to try and show that mental problems are seldom endemic to those afflicted, that their actual predispositional causation lies elsewhere—with other people who have conflicting interests, lifestyles, personalities. Many authorities on psychiatry, as well as the legal profession and social scientists, are increasingly in agreement that regarding modern society and mental illness, biological factors are of a reduced significance. In stronger ascendancy are social or environmental explanations. For life is our experience of other people around us and how we develop depends upon others; our quality of existence, how long we live, and the pleasantness or unpleasantness of *how* we live. However, before our examination of twentieth century modern societies, it is important to add some qualifications concerning the length of time mental disorder has been recognized, that it is certainly not exclusively a product of the last century. Attempts to understand insanity and misunderstandings of it are as old, perhaps, as the hills. It is vital, therefore, to look through a historical perspective to give some framework of analysis as well as to hopefully shed more light upon a still greatly unresolved problem. Or to put it another way if, as people today state that they still cannot understand much of the human mind and have had all human history in which to attempt to do so, then we can soon see that we are presented with a highly intractable task. Is there some very simple, perhaps elusive, reason for what we have hinted at above? Namely, that we may have (especially medical persons) been looking in the wrong place. Is the focus on the human brain per se something of a mischievous red herring? How about us instead looking at societies and their power structures, shifting laws and gaping inequalities embedded in cultures of contradictions? That is, testimonies to the fallibility of humanity, within which seeds sown of injustice give direct or indirect consequences for the mental quality of life for its inhabitants.

Chapter 2

A Confused Legacy

Rockets may land on the moon, shuttle probes may be sent out to fathom the more distant reaches of our solar system, and telescopes peer yet deeper into the void. Yet a lot closer to home a different kind of universe still stubbornly goads us, for our ignorance of even its most rudimentary workings: the human mind. Modern sophisticated technology and highly advanced life sciences still cannot confidently confront such an enigma. The X in the equation is still a virtually insoluble unknown and yet the above remark might at first consideration seem rather unfair; after all, we are more informed of such matters as emotions, feelings, cognitive states, and their causation. Indeed, there is quite a lot that psychology, psychiatry, and other social sciences can reveal to us about many aspects of how the mind functions. We know, for instance, that great tiredness can lead to irritability or the loss of a spouse to a crushing, cramping assault on one's previous contentment. And, of course, we are well informed and can deal better now with physical malfunctions such as cancer or major organ transplants. It would be extremely narrow-minded as well as grossly incorrect to state that the medical field has not made quite astounding advances in its knowledge-ability in health of both the body and the mind. All right so far, but when we come to consider sudden mental disintegration, and the white hot cauldron of controversy of its precise causation, then our telescope no longer seems to possess sufficient power to probe any further.

It is not so much that there are several explanations of worthlessness for all may contain valuable intrinsic use pertinent to each of them; rather, it is precisely that they have for millennia irreducibly competed with one another with very little mutual empathy and little common ground. None have achieved ascendancy, more seriously none have clearly demonstrated significant practical applicability. This is the main worrying element. Nothing is more certain to dampen one's enthusiasm than an argument between top specialists which ends in utter disagreement. To listen to such a debate makes it quite clear that confusion is the hallmark of the whole agenda. Ambiguity in mental health hierarchies is invariably the name of the game. Psychiatry only rarely uses precision or a sense of exactitude as one of its instruments—unlike, for instance, cardiovascular surgery. The difficulty seems to stem from an inadequate conceptualization of even the most fundamental things or what exactly is and should be the primary focus. What is it the medics wish to actually do? Then there is the disputed ethicality of should they do so? When, where, and upon whom? And in a wider perspective—just why should the procedure be applied anyway? For if it is so that no clear opinion as to a definition of normality has hitherto been arrived at, then how can abnormality be confidently and respectably diagnosed? Treated? What are medics trying to actually remedy, solve, resolve? Who is suffering? Who has the authority or power to say a person's way of thought should and can be changed? And changed to what, we might wonder? This really opens up an enormous Pandora's box, but essentially a quite recent one—spanning roughly the last 150 years. Obviously, people have been aware of such matters for a long, long time. What is distinctively novel, unique, in fact is the actual approach to mental disorder which has proceeded hand-in-hand with a rationalistic modernity since industrialization began. The intertwining of science and philosophical thought has given a springboard to an essentially novel, new way of approaching mental health. Thus, in centuries past, madness undoubtedly did exist, people suffered from it, and others noticed it—let there be no mistake about that. Our forebears were not unaware intellectual philistines. The point is, simply, that they approached things in a different way—to fit in with their civilizations, cultures, events, modes of thought as particular points in space and time—their eras. History straight jacketed their conceptions and assumptions, not in a delimiting way constraining powers of intellect and reason, but in a deterministic way of being located at earlier points in human history; they were denied (as we are not) greater opportunities of retrospection. Hindsight is always a good way to forget qualifications of superiority, to cheat one's predecessors. So let us now usefully point our telescopes not into the future but into yesterday, to see what legacy the past has bequeathed us in the shifting sands of mental health.

Sweeping across Europe in the eighteenth century, having its seeds in the enlightenment movement, was a raging thirst not simply for greater knowledge but a more precise accumulation and methodology of investigation. This fervour way pre-eminent in the physical sciences and the entire edifice of this hive of learning could be found under an umbrella of what has been called positivism. Basically positivistic thought implied not simply a search for more knowledge of the natural world but it crucially contained a built-in desire to foresee; to predict. A form of attempting to arrive at causal explanations by deduction, it followed from this that if the community of scholars were in agreement over a proposition then laws could be thence established. It was agreed, therefore, that developments could forever be predicted, acted upon whatever for all the future.

Accompanying this intellectual ferment in the physical sciences was an equally enthusiastic attempt to apply positivist enquiry not just to inanimate matter but to human beings. A great dream lay behind this of the ultimate possibilities of social engineering. Apart from any difficulties that positivism posed for physics and other natural sciences, it was to lead to a massive field of debate and disagreement—the embers of which still glow furiously hot to this day. For when attempting to formulate laws or hypotheses about such an incredibly complex thing as human consciousness, vast problems arise. Even seemingly fundamental questions—such as why minds construct wonderful if unrealisable utopias or devise horrific weapons and wars—caused great headaches for the ambitious positivist school; surely it might be that humans are the most rational, understanding, and advanced of all living species. It is precisely the fact that irrationality may be as great a motivating principle in human behaviour as rationality that constituted such an awkward conundrum for positivism. Its apparatus of logic could not easily accommodate phenomena of an essentially illogical nature. In fact, coming to terms with irrationality (of which, incidentally, mental disorder has taken a central place) was not seriously taken on board throughout much of the early insatiable desire for knowledge in the positivist enterprise. Nonetheless, the bargain struck. Social scientists, ranging from philosophers to economists, psychologists, sociologists, and political scientists, all got rapidly sucked into a system of wanting to know more and crucially—the desire to measure, to tangibly quantify what posed as its subject matter, the highly elusive problem of subjectivity. So much so that if a healthy *normal* mind created vast difficulties to comprehend, then the tortuously difficult state of an unhealthy, *abnormal* psyche really put the spanner in the works of the positivists endeavour.

As was pointed out above, it is very easy, possibly unfair even, to look back with a critical, often intolerant kind of perspective. For it may well be the case that future generations may look back at us, at our intellectual output, with elements of amusement (even mockery and disdain) at what they might conceive to be our idiocy and stunted powers of reasoning. This being the case, we need patiently to look back at the positivists and their work to see just what they were trying to grapple with and if their methods of enquiry in any way enhanced their insights into mental health.

In later chapters the focus will shift away from an emphasis of looking at the human mind per se, breaking away from rather deterministic, organic theories. We will take a look instead at processes of modernity and social changes of worldwide influence, especially since industrialization and urbanization. These twin latter developments, it will be argued, have instilled an atmosphere of a particular kind of human mentality which is not so much *abnormal* in itself, but acts as an adverse predispositional influence on people's quality and perceptions of their experience. This is not to tediously rehash the old nature/nurture controversy and unhelpfully attempt to collapse polarized explanations into some comfortable middle ground. Such attempts have been done successfully, if rather pointlessly (even nauseatingly) for most of this century. For such efforts to achieve the impossible harmony of exactly equal biological and social equivalents seem more intended to keep the peace amongst the two disputing camps than as a serious attempt at resolution of the problem. The intention here is to try and break new ground; by simple logic, moving forwards is impossible if only by a duplication of existing knowledge of sideways moves. Such repetitions in the literature have, as actual modes of explanation, possessed elements of a frustrating circularity principally because their analysis has only utilized static causal variables. However, if instead, dynamic processes—that is, ongoing unstoppable influences on human populations coupled with unique changing societies—is the stuff of our analysis, then we cease to deal with statistics and begin to deal with real people, who move, think, imagine, feel. Only by approaching human beings as they actually and exactly are (in contrast to sterile hypothetical typologies of how they might or should be), will any real and lasting advances be made in the field.

So often in social science research frameworks, people have been simply slotted into a design to contain them, when arguably they should have been the object of scrutiny first; that is, should have preceded such frameworks. To illustrate one crucial part of social change, we can point, for instance, to the eighteenth century landless labourer, who in the actual method of evaluation at the time was classed *not* as working class, neurotic, or unemployed, but as a member perhaps of the "dangerous classes," either feeble-minded or just an idiot, a lunatic constituting an unwarranted encumbrance on society. For him or her the place of stay would often not be a hospital, but instead a workhouse. There exists different perceptions of people's mental states at different points in history, coupled with often quite

13

different mechanisms of causation of illness and crucially differential degrees of sympathy, empathy, and tolerance.

Positivism ambitiously, despite its many internal wranglings, entered the field of what was a loose mass of ideas to later crystalize into what was to become psychiatry. And it was mainly within western Europe, in the late eighteenth century and early nineteenth century, that such developments both eagerly took root and then flourished. In fact, it was in Italy that the first moves towards a scientific approach to mental illness were made, with what seems to have been a quite humanitarian morality. Does this imply that before the positivist a non-humanitarian, even possibly cruel approach, may have prevailed? Well, from the historical evidence, the answer appears to be a categorical yes. For it could be agreed that an utterly different attitude was apparent. Whether by having one's limbs hopelessly dislocated on the rack or one's tongue ripped out, ears cut off, or forehead branded by a red hot iron, mental disorder was clearly not looked upon by moral guardians of the day in a benign, benevolent manner. Illness was seen as something to purge out of the mind; to be banished, tortured away. This is because it was widely believed that insanity was synonymous with demonological possession. It was viewed as intimately associated with devilry, satanic manifestation, a hideous possessiveness of wickedness that had to be dealt with appropriately. At the time, especially in the middle ages in Britain, insanity was barbarously expelled at all costs. The madman then thus suffered needlessly excruciating pain as his/her "treatment" programme, unlike today sitting in a cosy armchair in a psychotherapy group.

So that initially it was in Italy whereby Cesare Lombroso, a physician of positivist endeavour, came up with what now seem highly antiquated, even perhaps bizarre, theories. This was mainly due to the core of his opinions that certain mental states could be accurately deduced from physical observation of the human body, anatomical morphology, not physiology was the salient variable. More accurately, Lombroso contended that there was, dependent upon one's physical characteristics, a definite criminal type. Hence, particularly large people or those unfortunate enough to possess jutting jawbones, large skulls, or ears that stuck out, got caught in the suspicion of the doctors net of having a deviant personality. Of course, nowadays such schemes may strike us as ridiculous for we no longer evaluate people's actions solely upon their physical morphology. Indeed, much of the fallacy of Lombroso's work was revealed in its empirical application. Many of his typical, classic types did not show any propensity to deviance, whilst many people that did not fit into the ideal, typical

14

classification *did* become criminals. This is just one of the kinds of error made in the early positivist school, that of untested presuppositions leading to grandiose, sweeping conclusions with no research in between having been performed. And yet the consequences were not merely an embarrassment for clinicians. There were victims, real people suffered—the patients. Those deemed to resemble the typical criminal type were bombarded with bizarre "cures" in order to prevent them supposedly sliding irresponsibly into a fully fledged criminal career.

All grim stuff. And yet were not the developments in early British asylums a century later any less draconian or grotesque? For indeed, it was the case that a person who claimed to be hearing voices would be strapped securely down onto a revolving table and then whirred round and round at a considerable speed way past the limit of discomforting dizziness. The aim, should the unfortunate subject not have suffered unconsciousness or brain damage in the process, would be to try and get blood to rush to the head so as to supposedly clear the mind from confusion and give it nourishment. This "treatment," like many others, took a long time to wane. But just whether or not such physicians who authorized these therapies were to actually blame is very difficult to say. For to be fair to them, they were acting upon the very limited knowledge that was available at the time. So that they were no doubt unashamedly convinced, at the time they practiced, that their methods of both diagnosis and treatment were entirely appropriate.

In fact, when such strange activities are revealed to us on our television documentaries today, we may well give a wry smile, yet at the actual moment the practices occurred it was no doubt a very serious business. The amusing side could be the young lady who, in nineteenth century England, complained of urban claustrophobia, having been living in a smokey, industrial town. The person, soon to be a patient, disliked pollution and had an intense yearning for a place of uncluttered openness. The physician who happened to notice such desperate longings may have considered her condition possibly pathological, but quite a reasonable request for suitable help. Therefore, the necessary action would be to induce a remedy so as to let the poor lady have wide horizons of the very best of rural England. Hence, a birdcage containing live canaries would be fastened onto the top of her head, her arms tied to the chair. She would be blindfolded, then left alone undisturbed in a dark room for a couple of days. Eventually the doctor would come in, open the curtains, free her limbs, and remove the blindfold and cage of warbling birds.

"How do you feel now?" he would ask pleasantly, but with genuine concern.

The woman, albeit a little drowsy and confused, would nonetheless state quite honestly and happily that she had just had a wonderful experience.

"I've just been in the countryside, doctor, so peaceful listening to the sound of lovely, beautiful singing birds."

"So, you feel happier, more relaxed, content?" he would ask her.

"Oh, yes, doctor, so much happier now," she would say, feeling refreshed and full of sunshine, with clear eyes and refreshed vigour.

Funny now perhaps, but for some people who were patients, not quite so funny. Their experiences were far more austere and unpleasant. For instance, one of the classic opinions held by nineteenth century doctors was that of the apparently great therapeutic benefits to be gained from putting patients in total isolation: solitary confinement, or seclusion, as it is now called. One doctor in Broadmoor Hospital in Berkshire was most definitely of this opinion. He felt quite adamant that a patient, seemingly disturbed, would find it greatly advantageous if he or she were placed entirely alone in a small, locked room for several weeks, even months—sort of a "as long as it takes" procedure. This method was felt to help the patients to collect their thoughts, get things into order, perspective. During the confinement, the patient would not be allowed to talk to anybody or even leave the room, the room consisting of solely a mattress on the floor and a chamberpot. Meals would be passed through a small open-shut panel in the steel bolted door. "Success" of this procedure or otherwise would be entirely the prerogative of the doctor, who possessed a virtual monopoly of clinical decision making, or treatments for patients. This is synonymous with saying that doctors largely controlled both patients' lives and their everyday quality of life. Patients' futures were the doctor's concern whilst ever they remained under his power within towering hospital perimeter walls and gates of Victorian iron.

Other patients deemed to require "treatment" would simply just be "bled"—the procedure for supposedly bad or disease-ridden blood: The mad were thought to possess a blood disorder as a result of being mentally unwell. So, it was thought, if the blood could be drained the patient would improve mentally. Other patients faced a different treatment scenario— water therapy. They would be tied up and placed in baths of freezing cold

16

water whilst a tank of equally cold water rested just above their heads. At the instruction of the doctor present, an asylum attendant would pull a chain and a cascade of water would be unleashed down upon the head of a patient who, already by virtue of the bath alone, had almost involuntarily contracted pneumonia. Once again, judgement as to the effectiveness of this treatment was in the capacity solely of the doctor. It was not the patient's opinion that mattered, for that counted little at all. If the doctor thought it was doing the patient good, then there would be plenty more cold baths to come.

And yet, incredibly, such methods of managing the mad were, in contrast to earlier times, very humane. The seventeenth century lonely widow who kept a couple of cats and a raven in a cage in her house was most certainly seen as *abnormal*, not to be treated but persecuted. So often it would be the case that a ducking stool would be the remedy for the lonely biography she had chosen to live, only to be made to drown as a consequence.

We can relate the above—that is, individual idiosyncrasies often being incorrectly misconstrued as posing apparent threats to society—too much of the theme of this book. In essence it is that certain people who wish to escape the shackles of a crushing conformity often end up labelled as *sick* or *abnormal* by legal and medical watchdogs. This has perhaps never been so important an issue as now. For, roughly since World War II and it cannot be dated any more accurately than that, there has been a staggering proliferation of the conscious desire to achieve a personalized status of "being different," not to any longer be just a cog in a big anonymous wheel of society's amorphous machinery. Side-by-side with this is a very marked rise in the proportion of the population in modern society being classed as psychiatrically unwell. The evidence reveals that far from the two variables being separate, they are most definitely inseparably intertwined. But the methods of investigation of the nature of their precise relationship is not at all an easy matter, because lots of other influences act upon them, alter them, complicate them. It is the unenviable task of the social scientist to investigate differential degrees of causation, in what is still a problem of a very little-researched nature. Indeed, as the early positivists found to their costs, human diversity is no close bedfellow of generalization.

The nineteenth century was certainly a watershed as regards the still fragmented but nonetheless slowly growing discipline of psychiatry. This is so mainly due to the reason that for the first time in history, institutions were specifically designed and set up for those perceived to be of unsound mind, even if still "dangerous idiots." Several acts began to appear in official legislation, in the middle of the last century, giving rise to the building of places such as Bethlem Star Hospital, more commonly referred to as "Bedlam." Such asylums used as forms of "care" predominantly physical restraint, for specialized drugs had not then appeared upon the scene, and were not to do so until almost a full century later. A.T. Scull documents such matters in his book, *Museums of Madness*, in which he argues that the development of psychiatry and management of the mad was not solely a province of medics. It was a hotly contested arena, with the ultimate prize being power and wealth, to win over the custody of lunatics in society. The contestants were not just doctors, but also lawyers, clergymen, and historians, all of whom perceived that they had a quite justifiable claim in the control both of clinical and administrative concerns of England's early asylums. This was accompanied by a rapid proliferation of legal statutes, such as the Mad Houses Act, Idiots Act, and other acts concerning those of feeble mind; all intended to exert custodianship over those afflicted. So that the mental hospital was born and accepted by society as a legitimate kind of organization, even if its aims or functions remained poorly understood. Closely paralleling the construction of the asylums came a slow but diminishing reliance upon the old "cures" or therapies. Thus patients were no longer bled or locked in rooms with birdcages fastened to their heads or given cold water "therapy." This was championed in the progressive political sphere of the day. A time for social reform accompanying changes occurred in areas like sanitation, housing, factory acts, mine acts, and many other areas also singled out for improvement. It was a time of activity to attempt to change what was seen as anachronistic in a developed, civilized society which many upper echelons felt was the case. For it was no good if the Great Exhibition symbolized progress in the material world if it was to stand embarrassingly alongside widespread social squalor in the new, teeming cities. Hence, improvements came whether consciously desired or not.

One aspect of the early asylums was their removal of inmates not only from mainstream social life, that is by locking them up, but also geographically. For there was a quite distanced spatial separation, with asylums often being built in the middle of nowhere, usually a long way from urban centres. Many not yet demolished bear testimony to this fact today. But again, there was a quite well-intentioned motive. It was explicitly to let patients have ample access to fresh air and countryside, to get them away from towns which were seen as having induced a disorderly mentality in many of them in the first place. A tenuous link was thought to exist between urban chaos, its disorganized rootlessness, and disorder in the town-dwellers' minds.

The leaders of nineteenth century England could congratulate themselves on seemingly sweeping away the ancient regime and sending forth endlessly rolling waves of humanitarian progress, and the asylum was a crucial element in this. Thus, the physical aide of madness management had been transformed but now we might ask ourselves—had its understanding? It is doubtful if it had improved to any great extent, apart perhaps from more sympathetic attitudes—people no longer ill and wicked, but ill and feeble-minded. There certainly appeared less victimization of patients, a reduction in stigmatization, but as to the crucial word of *understanding*, things are far less dogmatic. Whether people could be any more clear of specific about causes of mental disorder is a very open question. Leading on from this controversy is another, namely, that although new therapies were more humane were they any more effective at both "curing" a patient and also of preventing mental disorders from arising? This is a highly debatable question many doctors uncomfortably have to face even today. Still, the upshot is that there have been highly dramatic, worthwhile steps forward. Hence, if a patient claims to be hearing voices (auditory hallucinations), then today certain drugs do exist to often effectively reduce the distressing effects, even if an actual outright cure is (as it currently is) not available.

Such treatments did not exist until quite recently. Joan of Arc's voices were not psychiatrically treated or considered even suitable for psychiatric treatment; she was viewed as demonologically possessed, with fire being the only "cure." Here again we see psychiatric technique or method coupled with social evaluation of the nature of the problem. Both move, often uneasily, side-by-side through time. Another good example of just this fact is the Roman society's attitude to Jesus Christ. In the Roman's limited conception, not only did they totally reject claims of a divine nature of being perhaps the son of God. They also, even if this were not the case, simply attributed to him the case of a disruptive fraud. The word "delusion" did not exist in their social system. Their sympathy for his claims, his behaviour, was virtually zero; it was not just an attitude of disbelief but caustic distaste. To put it another way—anybody today claiming to be the son of God usually ends up in psychiatric care, whereas two thousand years ago a man making exactly the same claim was not nearly so lucky. Not only were his bold statements ridiculed and himself subjected to beatings and utmost humiliation for making such statement, he also received no empathy from those in power at the time. The action taken—cure, treatment, therapy, call it what you like—rivalled some of the cruelest ever devised; agonizing crucifixion.

Chapter 3

Indigenous Aliens

At the risk of pseudo science fiction, could it be remarked that human beings are growing tired of fellow earthlings? For undoubtably ranging from the staggering upsurge of computer games on sale in recent years, for a market focus of tots of two to pensioners, we see the explosion of a massive desire for diversions. In the cinema and most high streets we see stacked higher and higher on shelves videos of cosmic escapism. Initially it was "Battlestar Galactica" and the "2001 Space Odyssey." Now upon such early themes are constructed a plethora of thrills of defeating invaders from afar. So great is the desire for fantasy as contrasted to a mundane modernity in which we live! The expression upon our faces as we look at the T.V. is not passive boredom, nor even mild excitement; rather it is one of audio and visual intoxication. We are identifying with it, living it. Engrossment leads to almost participant interest, remote galaxies monopolize minds, starships are so much closer to our hearts and thoughts than the next door neighbour, our work place, shopping parade.

Why is such dissociation from the everyday taking place? Is it a fully conscious decision? In other words, are we getting a little bit sick and tired of other people who reciprocally show the same disinterest and indifference to us? Obviously, this is a sweeping, general, impersonal process. It doesn't by any means pre-empt close love in the romantic sense, but generally, it may be contended that more and more of us are in a whirling, confusing vortex of decreasing proximity to one another. This may be more than at any previous time in history; so that social life takes on the scenario of a differentiated strangerhood.

The above detour is merely an attempt to show that the substance of modern society seems for many of its inhabitants to be becoming increasingly routinized. That is, a greater infusion of predictability and with it a parallel disintegration through the remorseless elimination of surprises. People like novelty, and if it is removed, some replaceable form of stimulation may be required—hence, watching battles on Saturn or clashes of yet more distant Titans in distant galaxies. So if (and this by no means collapses everyone into the same viewpoint) we are tending to interact less in our immediate social milieux, then what can be cogently asserted is that such a *blase* indifference will serve as to be doubly damaging upon already existing schisms prevalent in society. Long entrenched grooves of anxiety will be reinforced by another coat of the same paint. Essentially—if we have already expressed, implicitly or explicitly, disdain for immigrants or those at the bottom of our stratification system, then a tightening of the belt of our exhausted reserves of empathy will lead to less tolerance for such subjects than was formerly the case.

Does this imply that people are getting meaner, narrower, and more insular and impatient with one another in an overall context of diminishing tolerance? This is a major philosophical conundrum in this peculiar age of modernity, which will be touched upon in Chapter Eight; it has simply served here as a backdrop against which other arguments can be located and thereby hopeful more clearly discerned. To review thus far then: we have looked at a few closely interrelated ideas of our contemporary existence and importantly we have seen that fundamental already existing cleavages or divisions have cut through false, comfortable doctrines, often proclaimed to be eternal—like universal love, democracy for all, equality for all. These have indeed been seen through by many of us and are less credible as a result. It is a situation of an unintended, unexpected circumstance accompanying social development which has had a detrimental superimposition upon already existing problems. Are such problems virtually beyond solution? Can people solve them, or is it the case that they are not prepared to do so? Such dilemmas lie at the centre of social science today. In fact, many debates do address such unresolved ones. Such tortuous difficulties were anticipated before this book was written, but the intention to nonetheless proceed was assisted by the tantalizing notion of a largely unrecognized and little used possibly new perspective.

But enough of theory for the moment and a need for a more *factual* tone. Theory *is* still needed if only to give a kind of framework to arguments which follow. This is vital, especially when there is a need to confront influences upon our behaviour such as perceptions of fairness, a sense of ostracism, deliberate ignorance, compassion, cruelty, selfishness, and people's nebulous justifications concerning their own status amongst one another. All such things exist within ideological contexts and myths and doctrines we have been indoctrinated with, often without even having realized it. One offshoot of this is that we often assert our believed originality of individualism so as to desperately separate ourselves from others that we don't wish to associate with or be bracketed alongside. This is, in ways, a curse insofar as it squeezes out much of the potential for discussion. People are fragmented with separate solutions to their (essentially very similar) problems, at just the moment of a much-needed unification. Another way of saying this is that it is not that a single human mind cannot grapple with key modern problems. It is rather that a solution to present problems is frustrated by lack of a communal agreement—due to disparate wants as a result of disparate lifestyles. Let us probe these woolly terms now and anchor ourselves in some specifics.

It has already been remarked that certain divisions exist and persist in virtually every nation worldwide—those of class, race, and gender being particularly prominent. A far more insidious, often unrecognized, and little-explained division is quite simply that between those classed as mentally well and those designated as mentally unwell. This important fact is often omitted in most so-called modern, comprehensive textbooks or, at most, dealt with only very superficially. This may be due to a dearth of existing work on the subject or it may be that the actual cleavage between ill/not ill does not warrant the social scientists' approval of what constitutes a societal division. But even on quick reflection it can soon be seen that it most certainly is. Indeed, we are being very sociological here. For the whole enterprise of sociology is to use an imaginative, insightful scalpel to remove, clear away, so much that passes as *common sense* or *truth*—that is, to uncover the familiar to reveal the unfamiliar which often surprisingly alerts us to take the revelation that what we took as perfectly *normal* or *natural* is nothing of the sort, that it could have equally been quite otherwise the case. That it was not, that is the reason things remained unclear and mysterious, unexamined, was because certain social actors found it to their advantage to keep things in the dark; furthermore, they didn't allow it. And yet human volition, despite its often limited powers of expression from structurally induced constraints may not, on deeper thought, be so selfish at all.

For it was mentioned above about our manipulable consciousness, our social molding, our susceptibility to ideological indoctrination. Even if not totally brainwashed, we do unreflectingly, unknowingly absorb a lot of things we would most certainly avoid or reject were we not so unfortunately malleable psychologically.

Certain stereotypes of the mentally ill that we possess are not our own creations, they are instead collectivized, ingrained, stereotypical impressions foisted upon us. They are present in society—a place in which we spend our entire lives, desired or not. We are often unavoidably the unwilling subjects of certain socializing processes which we have been powerless to resist. To have resisted, were it remotely possible anyway, would have been regarded as nonconformist, even deviant; alternatively whilst the socializing process was occurring we were unknowing of how this would eventually be one day acted out; that is, affect our future attitudes, our behaviour. This is not to provide an automatic excuse for us possessing often an undesirable imagery or wrong attitude to the mentally unwell, but simply to say it is not always people's fault to actually harbour such a stereotypical picture. We are not biologically programmed with blueprints of suspicion, dislike, scorn, and lack of sympathy towards those who, in our midst, are less fortunate in their powers of mental faculties. Rather, we have subtly—through several sedimented layers of socializing agencies—been transformed to possess certain, non-genetic, non-inherited traits. We have learned to possibly be racist, egocentric, non-altruistic. Indeed, biology or heavy genetic theory is often used to justify all sorts of injustice, whereas in actual fact it is the learning process, post-birth, which is the dominant influence.

So that even mental illness can conveniently be attributed to biology, and this will be challenged in the pages which lie ahead. Such biologically derived explanations serve both to oversimplify the problem, and more damaging still, actually *justify* a continued negative towards the mentally ill. It is justified as "biologically born and forever made" by certain social groups because it is in their interests to do so. More specifically, such groups do not desire a greater understanding of the social causes of illness; non-genetic explanations are not wanted, even though they may well be crucially important, for their discovery and widespread disclosure could upset a lot of contemporary comfortable apple carts. The status quo is often very attractive to some.

Now above it may have appeared that sympathy was felt for people who possess stereotypical visions of mentally ill people, but only to a limited extent does such a reservoir of sympathy extend. For now the time is due to criticize perhaps not so much the public, but rather the actual agencies of such dissemination of misleading, incorrect information about mental ill health, and those who succumb to it. After locating the sources of mythology we then can look at the consequences for those whom we (wrongly) perceive to have departed from a *normal* healthy state of mind. Those, unlike ourselves or so we believe or crucially, who are *led* to believe by our incessant societal conditioning.

We must now unmovingly focus on the modern mass media. Arguably, before the arrival of the modern mass media, our misperception of the mentally ill and especially the deviant mentally ill were never so sharply defined as today. Whereas in the middle ages, with its lack of an almost instantaneous electric communication system, people who acted strangely were dealt with locally, that is highly specifically, to an almost total ignorance of the rest of the population. Punishment meted out was specific, let us say a dozen lookers-on by the village pond ducking stool, and nobody else knowing much about it. This is completely different today. The whole essence of the criminally insane is brought into the minds of thousands, even millions of us. The faces of "the mad axeman" or the "sexually depraved pervert" stare up at us at the breakfast table as we browse through our daily tabloid. We hear of such events on the radio, both hear and see it in our living rooms via the television set. Little is secret in modern society when it comes to newsworthiness, and madness is forever newsworthy. Just why this should be so is an interesting question subsequent chapters will explore. The whole notion of madness is what many people wonder about with fear and sometimes uneasily contemplate whether it could be happening to themselves. The key to this convoluted kind of anxiety is that madness is so perpetually an elusive thing. Nobody really knows exactly what it is or feels like or how it can be avoided, or how it is exactly caused. For this very reason of its refusal to be delineated—that is, recognizably pinned down and made rationally understandable in everyday terms and logic—it perturbs so many of us in a constantly nagging, uneasy way. And feel uneasy we most surely do with few of us desiring the label of mad or crazy ourselves.

It is precisely here that we may have within our grasp some very important insights into mental illness. Not just narrowly of the actual patient, who happens to be so afflicted, but also the opinions of those who are not, and why their interest is so persistently high and enduring. Let us therefore examine this in close conjunction with the mass media and hopefully a close relationship will be seen to emerge one previously assumed not to pertain.

It will be recalled that this chapter began with a consideration of a desire for distractions or fantasy in contemporary society, which revealed many people in hot pursuit of endless technological diversionary activities. This was then linked with a notion of separateness from one's own fellow beings. From this postulate we can now advance a further hypothesis—that regarding mental illness, much of modern social life is a paradox par excellence. That is, that people don't want to be involved with or shoulder any responsibility or obligation towards those deemed to be sick. Yet at the same time they have an intense interest in it and like incessantly more knowledge about it. This they are enabled to do through the avenue of the media—in newspapers, television, magazines, radio, and video. The question now raises its stubborn head: why should people be so inquisitive about something that they do not want anything to do with or interact with the actual people afflicted?

The reasons are many, some more obvious than others. Firstly, in many peoples' conceptions, mental illness is a terrible thing to contract; one classed in this category may well be propped up by pills, may be in an institution, classed as irresponsible and unsuitable for normal life outside. Madness also carries an unestimatable amount of social stigma; the last thing anyone wishes is to be mad, or be even considered mad. Now we are getting close to a crucial but subtle psychological defence mechanism; to live in social reality is such a delicate, precarious experience that people require constant reassurance. They need to feel this themselves and be told by others in a lifelong corroborating way, that they are *normal*.

Each person wants badly to know the answer to two closely connected questions; firstly, "Is the social world *normal*?" Well, the media tell them most certainly that it is not, that some of us are insane. This directly lets us know that it is not a *normal* social world, which critically makes us ask the even more important second question; "In the social world in which I live, am I *normal*?" This is the decider, the fulcrum of one's very psychological survival and self-esteem in the eyes of others (who equally are requiring exactly the same reassurance themselves). Now, if a scapegoat (this existence and actual visible presence of a mentally ill minority in society) is available, that is identifiable, a handy solution appears possible to the two above questions which we always worryingly pose to ourselves. For we can point the finger at the mad and simultaneously tell ourselves that we are not the same. Our own feelings of insecurity and inadequacy are magically erased, for we say to ourselves, they, the mad, and not I, possess such unwanted characteristics. That is, "I'm all right, but some others (the mad)

26

are not." This is very crucial to our feelings of social stability in the community, for as stated above, to contract insanity is to be at the ultimate whipping post of ridicule.

Now the above mechanisms of mentally well self-assuagance are only really possible to occur and persist, that is be reproduced in an ongoing fashion, by the existence of our modern mass media. If this did not exist, people would be far less confident of their lack of susceptibility to mental disorders. Hence, the media's manufacturing of scapegoats through a sensationalized filter is positively functional for the majority of the public's psychological stability. Not only are the ill disadvantaged by the handicap of actually being ill, they suffer a double misfortune in being *used*. They are used for the benefit of so-called *normal* people (the majority) who stigmatize them, regard them with suspicion, distaste even, don't really pretend to understand them or want to help them or know them; yet irresistibly need them purely for indirectly self-centred motives of individual self-gain. The actual process of media presentation, the *normal* public's reaction, needs a new and perhaps deeper analysis.

Often, as is the case in much modern media reportage, there tends to be a posing of what is to be considered a problem, in terms of extremes. A black or white kind of choice is made available to us from which we seem compelled to have to choose only one or the other. Intermediate gradations are not open—those that could, if present, indicate some flexibility, sensitivity in our opinion—such options are not open; it's just one extreme or the opposite extreme. Our discretionary room for manoeuvre is grossly restricted, which fits in nicely with the intention of the media agency who deliberately intended this to be so. In the classic presentation to us of criminals in the tabloids of the "Is he mad or is he bad?" question, we are left to inflexibly side with the writer. Also, the sick criminal has a highly emotive description, being labelled as a "fiend," "beast," or "maniac." Straightaway we have little choice but to stare down at our newspaper at the sinister silhouetted criminal who should (the paper argues) be removed forever from our recognition as suitable for an existence amongst us in the normal world. For, the account states, that person, the evil transgressor, is simply no longer sane like we are, and should thus be permanently removed from our midst. There must be no room, no quarter for aliens, in our apparently normal, healthy, law-abiding society. Furthermore, in the actual reportage, very little information (and certainly very little corresponding sympathy) is given as to what actual circumstances may have precipitated the mental breakdown. There is little mention of perhaps a stressful antecedent biography or poverty; instead, ninety percent of the report is on the actual offence committed and this is given a supposed legitimate stamp of being unexaggerated by the inclusion of a comment by a police or other legal spokesperson. Metaphorical language, given bizarre twists, puts the seal on it all: a crazy evil crime by a crazy evil perpetrator. The implication is clear that the creature responsible must be removed from our midst, not just because they are ill, but evil and ill.

All of the society's wrath, prejudices, and insensitivities are piledriven onto that photo on the front page of our popular national conscience—the daily newspaper. Pictures of victims alongside the criminal have meek, innocent, smiling, bright expressions on their faces, whereas the assailant has a deliberately shrouded, evil grimace. Readers look down at that face with a sign of blissful relief of "Thank God that's not me." This implies that up to press our sanity and righteousness are still preserved. We are relieved to realize that we are still sane.

Yet if a purely factual account were to have been the order of the day, it is unlikely the media would have sold as many newspapers; people would have been bored by a more open and honest account—a small readership for the presentation of the true, full facts of the matter, a massive readership for a largely fictitious story. Here we see the amazing, sad ironies of a sane and civilized society, as its members so adamantly believe is so. But once again, can it really be said that it is the public's *fault*? For as touched upon previously, people live in an insecure reality and constantly require a reaffirmation of their own mental stability and sense of law abidingness. Thus, through the channel of sensationalized accounts of insane criminals, people can avidly titillate their whims and prejudices, reaching in this way the only possible verdict—guilty and crazy. It is almost as if the popular media need to manufacture sensationalism so as to help keep well or secure those who have not yet succumbed to mental disintegration. Therefore, in order that group life, which is what social life is, does not break apart or splinter into a state of chaos, some people must, unfortunately, be used (in a manner disadvantageous to themselves) to ensure the continuation of the stable existence of the majority. Quite simply—society needs criminals, and it equally needs the mentally ill. For the irony is that without them, there would be far *more* mental disorder and crime than currently exists.

Rounding up our discussion, so far we have entered what is at the centre of key debates today in social science. We began by discussing many people's current inclinations towards fantasy and argued with some amount of persuasion that this was a desire for a form of nebulous escapism. But then the focus was sharpened somewhat, and given a factual foundation, when we observed the way that such a disinclination for our fellow human beings would doubly affect, in a deleterious way, those for whom we *already* have a limited tolerance; those we either ignore or steadfastly refuse to associate with. Such groups loosely include immigrants, the very poor, and many females in society. All of these groups having corresponding status devaluations in many people's estimations. But we also considered a group much neglected in social health studies—the mentally ill. It was found to be the case that the need for separation into an "us and them" continuum possessed the paradoxical quality of a dialectical relationship. This is that most *normal* people don't want any association with those labelled as *abnormal*, but that their ongoing psychological survival requires that the *abnormal* continue to flourish and be reproduced as part and parcel of the social system. We then looked at the useful function of the popular mass media in continually highlighting, and bringing to our attention on a daily, sensational basis, *abnormal* members of society. So that what superficially we might regard as trashy reports has an important, if irrational, function of maintenance of stability for social groups and, ultimately, society itself.

Where does the foregoing chain of analysis lead us? What conclusions emerge? It would appear to be that not only has the public's understanding and empathy towards mental illness advanced nowhere, but that it has nose-dived into a state of regression. For let this point be clear: With this particular social schism it is *not* a situation of stalemate perpetuated unchanged through time, it is a dynamic one. One which, if anything, is taking us backwards in our understanding or desire to do anything about it. It is the *free rider* problem; essentially that each individual assumes that *somebody else* will confront the problem and do something about it. The problem here, however, is that somebody else is thinking exactly the same, namely that someone else will act instead. The outcome of a *free rider* situation is that, in the end, nothing gets done; the problem is not solved, only prolonged and worsened.

The very last impression the preceding remarks are intended to convey is that of a ruthlessly self-centered humanity or, more exactly, a selfishness naturally endemic to them. And yet what is being argued and will be examined in detail later is that there are certain social, economic, and political currents actually at work in our modern age which predispose people to act in often callous and indifferent ways. So often it is not so much an individual's fault but rather an accumulation of unfortunate circumstances with people having insufficient time to perceive them and resolve them satisfactorily en mass—i.e. as a collectivity. We live in what has been termed a global village, a single world society, mainly through technological advance in facilitating greater communications. Whether our ability to understand ourselves and others in modern life has advanced side by side with progress in science, is a highly moot point.

Where all of this leaves the mentally ill is anybody's guess, but their plight does not conveniently disappear as a result. They still exist. Such a matter as to their futures will be looked at in detail later, but what now needs to be studied is a non-psychiatric explanation of psychiatric illness, a view that could well be snubbed and dubbed as "radical" psychiatry. It centres on variables like poverty, and not physiology; that is we are looking primarily through the sociologist's rather than the psychiatrist's frame of reference. It will though be necessary to take biological theory quite seriously as this, it will be argued, cannot be excluded. But now it is to a probing of socioeconomic variables that we must turn.

Chapter 4

Insanity and Inequality

Earlier it was seen that rarely is it possible to completely side with the innate factors responsible for mental ill health. Nor, however, is it possible to totally reject this and in the process be a total advocate of nurture causation; that is, environmental influences. It goes really without saying, therefore, that the debate has reached a strong state of academic impasse in stressing an amalgam of both nature and nurture. This fossilized conclusion is, to date, still apparent. Although this undoubtedly is a quite sound explanation, this does *not* necessarily mean that analysis should cease. Quite incisive insights can be gained by explaining in much greater detail both biological and social explanations. That is, an attempt to try and isolate the respective components and then synthesize these together is doubly fruitful insofar as it can then be applied to specifically different cases in which some of these causation influences may be of a differential significance. This chapter, as well as the next, lays greater emphasis upon social, economic, and political factors, but Chapter Six returns us to the genetic sphere. It will be seen that not only is existing work difficult to understand, but that even the actual problems addressed are little understood anyway. We may well be looking at a very old, long recognized problem, but it is still rooted in the very new ground of an unfamiliar land. But let us still see some enlightening glimpses made possible, so far, by social scientists.

Social theory can quite proudly put a feather in its cap for a long tradition of attempting to successfully isolate several processes at work producing social and subsequent psychological disintegration. Here the economy will be our centrepiece, whereas later on we will stress purely sociological and psychological methods of reasoning, some dating back a century or more with no rust gathered, their relevance as great today as then. Although it must certainly have occupied people's thoughts for many thousands of years—that poverty often led to a distinctively different

31

lifestyle as opposed to being rich—it has never been a unanimous agreement that poverty led to *mental* impoverishment, too. For quite rightly, as many skeptics of social explanations maintain, many people at the lowest of the low of our income stratification pyramid *never* contract mental illness, nor do they commit financially deviant transgressions. On the other hand, some very rich people, despite their abundant wealth, *do* commit financially motivated crimes. Why is this? As yet there is no clear answer, and it has often simply been the case that it has been left to individual idiosyncrasy, temptation, or moral weakness to engage, for instance, in corruption even though the money obtained from it may not be absolutely necessary. This is a very thorny, unresolved issue in social science—the big (not minor or marginal) exception to what logic would lead us to automatically assume about some apparently easily studied aspect of human motivation. There is a good reason for this. It is that human motives can often be as *irrational* as they are rational. This will be our focus later, but at the moment it might help if we consider some classical historical evidence written around the time of the industrial revolution in Britain, vividly portrayed by Karl Marx and Friedrich Engels.

First and foremost, it needs to be said that neither Marx nor Engels held any distaste for industrialization per se. What they *did* vehemently react against was a specific form of organization of industrialism in the shape of capitalism. What, for instance, Engels wrote about Coketown—that is, the sprawling industrial hub of nineteenth century Manchester alerts us to many things; for instance, the very basic fact that the appalling degradation and financial hardship endured by so many of early Manchester's inhabitants led to them developing symptoms of mental disorder—such as feelings of total hopelessness and despair. They were trapped in a system which they abhorred but could not escape from. Their poverty was their tyrant, ruling over every detail of their lives, dominating all things they would aspire to—adequate nutrition, sanitation, recreation, all of which were for many virtually nil. If the despair became too unbearable, (with no effective trade unions at the time), then the workhouse was the next stop. If anything other than money was lacking, it was sympathy by the more powerful sections of the community; sympathy was as thin as the layer of air spread upon the bread of those so despairingly afflicted.

So here the interesting question arises as to why there was no major revolt or even revolution as occurred in many other European nations. To a large extent, Marx provided an answer: His notion of religion being an opium of the masses; that is, a delusional drug, device, or palliative to hide the poor's immiseration. If heaven was believable as it was for so many of the disadvantaged, then they could (incredibly but certainly) put up with the hell of this life, this world's exploitative treadmill of dehumanization. They could wait for eventual heavenly bliss, and no longer be chained to the torture of the industrial clock and wheel. It could obviously be very useful to have possession of documents (which are largely unavailable) which could give some indication of the amount of mental illness prevalent at the time of such cataclysmic change as happened; to be able to understand how people fared or fell by the wayside, as mental hospitals were not sufficiently or adequately developed (or not even desired) to be part of the social infrastructure at the time. So that the edge of Marxist argument was that it was specifically capitalism which led to people succumbing to mental problems. This was because of the associated abject financial hardship of what was seen to be a totally unacceptable, evil system: specifically, and only that of capitalism. This view will be qualified in later chapters, where it will be shown that industrialism itself (encompassing all modes of production, consumption, and distribution) is, in the contemporary world, conducive to mental stress and a sense of uneasy disequilibrium for its peoples.

Marx never actually hypothesized any clear or direct linkage between inequality and insanity; these became later theorizations conducted in this century. Yet the type of observations and deductions he made and which we can usefully make provide quite strong evidence from which to proceed. One such theorist of recent times uses a mixture of Galbraith-style economics and radical sociology to try and show an almost sad inevitability of winners and losers in what is supposed to be a society composed entirely of winners. For the great American dream held out the unobtainable dream of everyone able to rise from "log cabin to White House." Idealistically, it seemed that if one put in enough hard work and matched such effort with the ability to shoulder responsibility, then riches and fame would be within easy reach. Crucially, of course, it missed out on one vital consideration; namely, that different people in society begin from situations of different opportunity chances. Some are already born into wealth and contacts (privilege by birth) whereas others (the disprivileged majority) are born into far less favourable financial circumstances. However, this was not the most valuable point. What was useful above all else in Robert Merton's work was that such avenues of blocked opportunity can lead to a sense of defeatism—throwing in the towel and just giving up, sliding into slum dwellings with permanently damaged aspirations, developing a lifelong closed mentality of neuroses. In fact, today research findings depressingly reveal that no less than a quarter of American society to be mentally ill.

Such evidence all ties in neatly with the above views of Marx and the dehumanization engendered by rampant industrialization. Marx used the concept of alienation to describe such a sense of estrangement from the work process, one's fellow human beings and, ultimately, oneself. It led to a fragmentation of feelings of human species, turning them into automatons. The work task and the entire nature of work, with its inexorable monotony, paved the way for a sense of and outlook of meaninglessness. Marx confined such a plight to just the working classes, and just to capitalism, but recent work sees industrialism itself as inducing the same self-degrading, stultifying effects upon human mentality. It is a complex mixture of sociology and economics, contained within a particular set of political doctrines or even philosophies, which are ultimately responsible for a state of alienation. Thus a resurgence of Coketown a century late can now be seen in many of our urban centres. This is because the same (laissez faire) kind of political views of how the economy should be organized have re-emerged. Such a perspective is in strong contrast to so many long established explanations provided by the biological school—cracks indeed beginning to appear in "organic" or "pathological" kinds of argument—so long paid lip service to, so seldom (until recently challenged.)

Usefully following on from above Marxist views are those of a far less radical nature provided by mainstream social theorists. Such workers in the field have no desire (unlike Marxists) to revolutionize society or transform it in a more egalitarian way. Their research findings possess an advantage of not being perhaps contaminated by bias or political praxis; that is, it tends to have impartiality, in *not* seeking to translate theory into action to change society. The findings indicate that the very poor (the lowest working classes) tend not only to have less material enjoyment, which is fairly obvious, but also suffer a great deal of mental impoverishment. They, when questioned in U.S.A. surveys, stated that they hardly ever go out, have very few friends, and have often sought, through sheer frustration and desperation, psychiatric help. They tend to be lonely people and unhappy, too. Now if we link this to what we discerned about Merton's earlier work about blocked opportunity due to different starting points, we can come to a rapid conclusion; namely, that in the race of social mobility it can be seen that the above survey respondents have had the rough edge of the American dream. It could perhaps be plausible to say that you can be part of a glorious affluent dream, healthy in body and in mind, be respected for it, providing you can afford that kind of status. If you cannot pay for it, then the dream is more of a perpetually uneasy, tension-riddled nightmare.

But of course as always, any potential ferment is already designed to be contained, rationalized, explained away. Or if any serious kind of turbulence is shown, it is controlled—such as by the state police, as in the Watts riots in Los Angeles, or the Chicago riots. Those rioting were the losers in the American dream, but it could not be officially disclosed that this was an unavoidable fault of a proudly proclaimed, ostensibly fair system. Dreams are meant to be happy, without any imperfections, hence the dream's perfection had, at all costs, to be upheld. Thus, reaction and disruption arising from widespread lower class discontent was violently repressed. So that the losers lost on both counts—denied participation in an affluent dream and imprisoned, or shot by police, for complaining. In a society whose ethos is about winning, losers really do lose.

Yet this is only to speak of advantages possessed financially. For although the material world does sift different income earners into different income areas, this is only a very obvious finding in research. For deeper under the surface we find the damage done has only just begun. This refers to the point at which different classes meet one another, or when similar classes happen to cross paths. Depending upon which, there will be either a disjunction in ease of communication, or a smooth rapport. This refers to class identities of those seeking psychiatric help, and the helpers—pyschiatrists (who tend to be of middle or upper middle class membership). Often a lot of common ground and ease of conversation exists between middle class patients and doctors, whereas this is not so often so with working class patients. A lot of similar kinds of experience do the same middle classes share in common, such as having had an extended education, secure upbringing, stable interesting employment, and social contacts. This tends not always to be so for the working class patient interacting in an interview situation with the doctor. There is a general atmosphere of strain, real rather than imagined; difficulty in trying to understand one another, mainly because socially they possess so little in common. Their respective biographies are different. For instance, the consultant finds it hard to empathize with the working class client who is redundant; that is, just *why* a state of being out of a job. Surely, the consultant feels, jobs are available for anyone who really tries to look for them, seeks out employment. What the consultant forgets is that his client may not possess (as he or she always does) lots of academic qualifications. This may be why the unemployed figure is without a job, particularly if this occurs during a period of economic recession. But there are so many other unfortunate misunderstandings that can follow from this. Night school may just not be a feasible or practical proposition for the working class client; more basically, there may be the fact that specific job skills once learnt are now no longer required—a victim of technological change. It may also not be easy to suddenly acquire new skills; the client may also be at an age when this is not viable.

In other words, different classes not only live in different material worlds, they more widely live different "life worlds"—of hopes, anxieties, prejudices, and above all, markedly different amounts of realism about what they feel they can and cannot achieve. Social class membership structures one's outlook, one's livelihood, one's life as a whole. Of course, there is quite a lot of social mobility—some working class lads do "come good," but this is an exception rather than the rule. For the majority of the working class, the really exciting things in life which are only tasted by a few are either very difficult to obtain through self help (that is, wholly through personal effort) or are denied.

The serious consequence of the above is that the middle class client is able to offer a picture to the consultant of *only* suffering from a *neurosis*, which is not a particularly debilitating mental handicap. This does not often pertain to the working class who are frequently classed as *psychotic*, which is a far more incapacitating condition with serious future implications for one so labelled. For example, the middle class neurotic may, as part of a treatment programme, take a small does of tablets, undergo a once-fortnightly chat with a doctor in a comfortable suite, the fees for which will not be too difficult to meet. Conversely, the working class client diagnosed as psychotic is placed in a very different, unfavourable position. The label "psychotic" often implies that the sufferer possesses lesser powers of volition, responsibility, logic, rationality, or control over behaviour. The actual day-to-day quality of life is hence quite tightly circumscribed. Indeed, such people are usually removed from everyday social life, being involuntarily incarcerated in an institution. The person ceases to be a citizen, taking on the status of mental patient. Just when he or she leaves the institution is invariably not their decision. Having being classed as psychotic, they have forfeited powers of rational decision making.

The power to make rational choices is transferred from the inmate to the doctor and nursing staff who comprise the medical team in charge of the patient's "care." Whilst in such a custodial setting, other undesirable events may occur in the form of supposed "treatment." These range from heavy doses of medication (some in the form of injections) to electrical shock "therapy" or even psychosurgery. Even more starkly, if it comes to the worst, some patients may never be released, having been in the hospital till the end of their days. Presumably they are seen as unfit or unsuitable to lead a *normal* life.

So that in preceding arguments several themes can be seen to be interconnected, all enmeshed in the relationship of poverty and psychiatric problems that stem from this. It has been seen that social class is a major determinant of one's quality of life, both physically and mentally. You can often literally purchase a happier existence and you can, if caught up on mental problems, buy or persuade people (largely due to your social class bracket) to obtain for yourself an existence of lesser or greater freedom whilst within the mental health net. But now a little bit of light will be added to the gloom of the above conclusions, to give a bizarre twist.

As we are aware, the human body and mind is extremely resilient; its powers to defy seemingly overwhelming adversity are amazing. For despite the appalling bring down in the lower class patient's lifestyle as he or she sits behind high walls, bars or windows for perhaps twenty years, there still exists an unusual but fascinating amount of leeway—even if it seems quite irrational or absurd. For paradoxically, although deeply enmeshed in the iron fist of the psychiatric syndrome and given virtually no recognition as a responsible citizen that is marginalized to the edge of society, the patient still has one last card to play. And in many respects it constitutes an *ace*. This card can still amazingly win the game. How, one might ask, is this remotely possible? Well, the situation here refers to psychiatric *delusions*— a false belief held by a patient to be of impeccable truth. So often a patient can be lying in bed in the middle of the night, having what in a way is the very last laugh. The patient can believe to be true that the very blame or fault for his or her demise was not their own fault at all, but was the work of devils of demons. *They* were to blame. So, according to this delusionally slanted logic, the patient is entirely guiltless, totally innocent.

Another perhaps even more amazing version of the exempt clause given by the possession of a delusional capacity by a patient is the belief of having divine powers. For it is the case that some patients believe one hundred percent that they are most surely and definitely God. The implications of them believing themselves to be God are fascinating. Thus nobody, not even the wisest of doctors, can persuade them one iota otherwise. No medication so far concocted, no treatment plan yet devised, can make any inroads into a psychiatric delusion. Delusional permanence, and its utmost realism and tangibility by one who possesses such a mental state, must surely be something reserved for those so massively degraded in status in this world. For it takes them *out* of this world, the very world which has labelled them *abnormal* and unworthy to live in. For they are, due to their magnificent delusion, effectively divine and thereby transcend this world and those mortals who were responsible for their incarceration in the asylum. Sweet, if strange, revenge? One might well wonder. For to be told one is insane is initially an enormous onslaught to one's dignity and pride. Enter now the delusion: This renders a rather special escape clause. It perhaps alerts all of us that in much of social life (as sociology shows) nothing is clear cut or straightforward; mental illness is certainly no exception.

Chapter 5

Blind Leading the Blind

Previously we suggested that rather than looking inward, using as a subject the human brain, the focus could be completely shifted to look outward at certain social and economic arrangements and political configurations of power at specific points in history. So that a constellation of interests in the complex matrix of societies could, with sufficient perceptive insight, reveal patterns of great unevenness of power, poverty, discrimination, and stigma. The latter concept is important as it often shows up to be a purely prejudiced ideological construct based not upon factual material but pure myth. So that by careful uncovering what in everyday life appears to be a for-all-time laid down naturalization of events, we can at last see that things could have been very different. If that is so, then it logically follows that many stressful or other environmentally mentally damaging influences could be removed. But this would only occur if there existed ample consensus in society and the political will to press the starting button of change.

Without intending to seem pessimistic, this is highly unlikely to happen—not so much because debate over the issue ends in confused disagreement, but rather because there is a lack of even elementary cognizance of what the issue to be debated actually even is. No objective yardsticks exist to measure, for example, the effects of long term unemployment. Some people go utterly to pieces, others don't. For the crucial explanatory variable predisposing some whilst others not is an enigma which cannot be put down to saying simplistically that some people possess greater resilience and stoicism than others. But this method of reasoning is not without a grain of truth. For essentially the enlightening vision here is to talk of predispositional influences acting upon a hitherto undamaged stratum of psychological susceptibility to stress. Yet even this is not a totally watertight explanation. This is because phenomena such as rapid economic development of secularization (debunking religious fervour in an absolute sense) drastically introduce complications into the equation. So that we can say that there is never ever a simple way of diagnosing mental illness either from the organic or environmental perspectives. But this does not aridly reduce us to the now cliched idea of "a mixture of the two," for it is now the juncture to inject into modern research work the usefulness of evaluating the relative strengths, not of actual environmental factors per se but their rapidity of appearance or disappearance. This is the job now urgently awaiting the social scientists; whereas genetics or, more exactly, the physical inheritance of mechanisms of one's vulnerability to later-in-life environmental stressful factors is more in the lap of the psychiatrist, or perhaps clinical psychologist.

For neither sociologist or psychiatrist is the task either easy or clear. It is very muddy waters. In many ways it is more difficult for the psychiatrist. This is above all so because the psychiatrist does not possess the ability to actually *see* the causes of what might be generating distress for the patient. For unlike physical surgery, whereby tissues can tangibly be placed upon slides beneath a microscope and looked at whenever it is desired, this is simply not possible when attempting to decipher problems of the mind. It is further complicated by the fact that the psychiatrist just doesn't know and perhaps can never know the exact turning point or moment when the stress-induced factors finally reacted with an organic weakness to push the patient over the edge. This limitation is a great pity, for if only we could know people's breaking points (that is, the time when the straw finally breaks the camel's back), we could prevent so much build up to illness, and nip it in the bud.

And yet the above is not only wishful thinking, it is illogical, too. For people all have different stress thresholds, different propensities to "going under." Also, of course, the strengths of the organically inherited factor are different amongst people regarding how susceptible it is to exogenous stress. But this is not to draw a full stop as so many researchers who have frustratingly thrown up their arms in despair have done about what they have seen as hopeless endeavour. For although the above argument may be quite true, it does not quite lead us to abandon our analysis—for one major reason. It is this: What has so far been called environmental inducements is *not* a diffuse set of factors which have necessarily held sway in any name of permanence throughout human history. Rather, it is a set of forces quite specific to industrial societies only really for the last two centuries. Such forces have accentuated organic weaknesses of traits perhaps inherited, or they have acted upon a non-organic base to still (through highly distinctive stress) create mental disorder, though this is not to say that before industrialization mental illness was non-existent. Clearly it was. But what is particularly novel is that the *amount* of mental illness since industrialism has been much greater. So that whereas in previous times people still suffered mental problems, it was not as anywhere near as substantial a scale or range across populations as it has been in the nineteenth and twentieth centuries.

Now we can proceed to see that it is the actual *intensity*, as well as the nature of pressures, which can act either on fertile psychologically inherited vulnerability or act on its own (on a kind of clean slate) to affect the frequency of inclination towards becoming ill. It is thus a particularly specific *kind* of society hitherto absent throughout human history which may well be responsible for such evidence, for example, that no less than a quarter of the United States population is currently mentally ill. Therefore, although it is probably a fruitless task to keep on arguing if mental disability is either innate or not, it *is* fruitful to try and identify, albeit in a rough and ready way, both the types of undesirable influences affecting as in industrial nations as well as their actual effects.

Such a way of exploring the above is to look at the problems by the comparative method; that is, in historic "now and then" terms. The "then" is preindustrial England, the "now" is the present time. What will be useful to identify is the rate or pace of change through these two periods by way of how people cope with or adjust, or fail to cope and adjust, with social change in too short a space of time for satisfactory psychological accommodation. That is, often rapid jolts to lifestyle and much altered relationships lie at the very core of change and our discussion of its unsettling ramifications.

Undoubtedly there have been three great interrelated processes of change at work in Britain which can be dated back to roughly (and roughly *is* the word, as sharp discontinuities are not apparent) 1850. It was a period which witnessed the demise of a previously dominant rural way of life. Agriculture had so long been the main enterprise not only in numbers employed but in its sheet intermeshing nature tying virtually all of the populace together. The countryside encompassed so many relationships bound together into a homogenous kind of system which today we cannot see or reconstruct in our much fragmented and dissociated set of institutions. The law was the law of the local parish, the church was in the village community and, most of all, relatively small urban centres functioned as military, ecclesiastical, or merchant hubs. The industrial conurbation of which we are now so familiar simply did not exist. What *did* exist was farming and a predominantly rural set of customary obligations in a hierarchy where people were far more certain of where they stood. That is, they were perhaps in a greater web of security concerning their day-to-day livelihoods due to a greater sense of intimacy.

Indeed, the sociologist Ferdinand Tonnies did some pathfinding work with his twin variables of *Gemeinschaft/Gesellschaft* which, loosely translated, means community/association. The former referred essentially to the past—the then, the pre-industrial, the pre-urban. On the other hand, *gesellschaft* stood for all that *gemeinschaft* did not. It epitomized a lifestyle of greater rapidity, a less enduring sense of closeness; people were strangers in a crowd. The crowd was ironically a mass of people but every one of its inhabitants was lonely; they hardly knew anybody else. This was because they were not able, due to the fluidity of the system, to get either the time, location, or opportunity to really get to develop any relationships of long-lasting consistence. Life was seen in *gesellschaft* to be so busy, so ephemeral an encounter. People could obviously see others but such contacts as ever ensued possessed a superficial fleetingness.

What Tonnies implied was an important statement about modern life generally being shaped by industrialization. What was unfortunately distorted his analysis has been that many subsequent researchers have quite incorrectly interpreted what Tonnies tried to say. They have wrongly posed *gemeinschaft* and *gesellschaft* with rural and urban as specific locational constructs; *where* people actually live. A purely sociological concept has been given an imprint of geography, and that is quite wrong if one is to stay true to Tonnies' original formulation. Highlighting this mistake is crucial to our analysis, for it is *not* the case (as has so mistakenly been supposed) that urban life per se induces one to mental disorder, but rather the pace, the speed of modern society generally.

The above argument possesses a great complexity covering societies worldwide, and not narrowly just Britain. It is useful in studying changes in many Third World countries which are undergoing industrial development. We may be able to correlate such changes with studies of rising problems of their respective populations' mental health. So that it is not so much the well worn hypothesis of dubious value that urban life causes people to become stressed. Instead it is the *process* of urbanization which

42

is the salient variable. It is therefore the degree to which long established habits or ways of life are changed which should merit our attention. For indeed, many people like city life, they enjoy it, take it at a steady pace, and never contract stressful or anxiety-provoked symptoms from living in the city. This may be because they are more fortunately endowed in being able to adjust to the transition or because though the city may be stressful for all its inhabitants, other pressures acting in conjunction with this may not have been apparent for those who are able to resist a neurosis.

So what we might ask: Are these other mysterious, detrimental influences at work which have accentuated the strains of living in an increasingly urbanized society? No doubt all sorts of answers might be forthcoming from different people holding different opinions—a reflection of their own specialism—but to eliminate elements of bias is to transcend the insular and side with a fusion of all of these; or, alternatively, to reject most or all of them and break radically new theoretical ground. Hence, many theorists keep telling us that there is a decline in religious adherence; this is a notoriously difficult topic which as yet is piecemeal and unsatisfactorily resolved. Tying in with the flavour of Tonnies' conceptualizations, it may be that a religious focus made the core of adherence to a commonly accepted set of values more firm, more rooted. That, instead of a serious splintering up into disparate activities; a structurally specialized system of differentiation. But the above "religion in decline" hypothesis is very doubtful and evidence to support it very dubious. It is a highly vague theorization, with no guarantee of establishing causation, to try to link a traditional decline of religious adherence to a sense of loss of intimacy in human groups. For we have little, if any, accurate information to employ in a measurable manner to enable us to gauge the intensity of religious fervour in previous times, especially if other nations were desired to be included in our problem. An international, or cross cultural, comparison would most seriously breach existing techniques of analytical research. This being a difficulty further compounded by the *nature* of the hypothesis—it is fundamentally an emotive or subjective topic and cannot thus be adequately fitted into an objective frame of reference. You might be able to measure people's behaviour, even their opinions, but their feelings are perhaps forever elusive, at least with contemporary methodology.

It may be impossible to attempt to evaluate the intensity of previous religiosity and compare it with the present. Nonetheless, religion has been demonstrated to promote a sense of solidarity in groups, and to that extent prevent many individuals from drifting into isolation with a lack of meaningful contacts with others. Thus the crux of the problem here seems to be to try and disentangle or separate out other variables with which the supposed religious "bonding effect" is inextricably intertwined. So we can easily come to appreciate that religion is a difficult topic to concretely analyze. Perhaps it can best be regarded not so much as a type of integrative ingredient but instead as just one of many examples of a generalized trend of splitting off of elements of custom or long-entrenched supports in the modern age. This can be viewed as a far wider growth of processes which have acted to transform both our social and material lifestyles. This is undoubtedly a global phenomenon associated with a rampant industrialism sweeping us along whether we consciously welcome such changes of not. Critically here, and challenging much of what passes for modern humanistic schools of Marxism, is the possibility that such societal disequilibrium which utterly refuses to be selective and is ruthlessly uniform across nations is not *capitalistic* in essence. It is to say that it is *industrialistic*, not a mode or particular kind of productive arrangement. Such things as profit, distribution, allocative mechanisms, and the like are essentially secondary in their importance of the context of our argument here.

So often we seem to be impersonally going about our business, irritated if another person gets in our way or obstructs us from our pursuits. But, what pursuits exactly, we might ask? The answer is a pursuit of blindness in a seemingly chaotic world increasingly and inexorably resembling a blind alley. And the previous handrails (or familiar paths that guide us) gave us a sense of purpose (direction), but they are becoming uncomfortably less familiar; they seem to be actually disappearing. Hence, a kind of obstacle race in a dimmer and dimmer arena, trying (as so many of us are though it is futile) to maintain the same sense of confidence, security, and stability we formerly possessed. What is more, those very supports we look to with greater and greater desperation, seem less convincing, blind themselves even. Governments themselves have, for a vast multitude of unforeseen reasons, contracted the same malaise—loss of vision, as those to whom they are apparently accountable. The human hive of activity is not only a busier one, it is a more confused one, too.

This links with previous arguments that, in a pre-industrial era, people's day-to-day lives had a much greater element of predictability built into them, even if at the cost of a humdrum monotony. The nub of it is that there was a social order without much of the machine, the technological chimes of an alien, amorphous clock, absence of remorseless routines. This was pre-industrialism. Familiarity with others, despite often a grinding poverty, did exist. Lives were less encapsulated in a nagging uncertainty. Customs, commitments, obligations were clearer and clearer to perceive, to adhere to, albeit even if codified in harsh (even draconian) regimes. It was the industrial clock plus the herding together in towns which heralded the seeds of our now apparently insoluble difficulties. People started, quite *unselfishly*, to paradoxically "look after number one," because so often for most it was becoming a sink or swim situation. This egoistic attitude also perhaps came about precisely due to the unfortunate fact that no single individual possessed enough time (literally lifespan) or knowledge of other people to imitate a *gemeinschaft* kind of relationship; this had to be rapidly, ruthlessly discarded in the rush for self preservation; this itself a microcosm of a selfish type of world. Human beings were becoming so enmeshed in their own problems, to the reduction of interaction with others, in exactly the same seemingly intractable position.

As the global village began to grow, it equally seemed to shrink in its intensity of contact or communion-like sentiments. The perceptive theorist George Simmel drew attention to this fact of the irony between greater human proximity and greater social anonymity. He looked at the way towns and cities often produced a blasé outlook of casual encounters of strangers in dense crowds. He further studied particular kinds of relationships and the emotional content of these as regards relationships with others. Indeed, the kind of urbanite Simmel portrayed could well be viewed by a psychiatrist as, at the very least, desensitized. The fact that people often when crossing the street deliberately look right through others, mirrors the transparency of the metropolis. With the cash nexus promoting an almost obsessional desire for holding tightly onto what one has already got (and desires to maintain) plus highly specialized impersonal institutional sectors of health, finance, or administration, we arrive at people ensconced in little worlds of their own. Yet lo and behold! The whole societal matrix of present horrific complexity is a wholly human construct! We have, and are responsible for our current isolated plight. What people voluntarily do (pure choice) turns out to subsequently ensnare them. And the lamentable thing is that later on people cannot see quite how it all occurred, they cannot rationalize their imprisonment of "how it all turned out this way."

One way of attempting to answer the kind of questions raised immediately above is to understand that there is no such thing as a "people's choice," a truly democratic, equal say for everyone in everyone's futures. Rather, it always tends to be that a few key personnel have a novel idea, and there is little effective opposition in reality to such ideas, often because at least in the early stages such ideas or plans are seldom disclosed (let alone publicly discussed). Such plans often achieve a momentum of a snowball effect, setting in train massive developments, industrialization being an excellent example. The whole argument here being that although the majority may have seemed to have benefitted from material developments—such as an escape from the worry about where the next meal is coming from—there has been quite a drastic downturn in many people's well being. People often feel less sure, less certain today. This is because rapid, seemingly unexplainable, change has rendered us with a sense of incessant relativism. Things are constantly compared, contrasted; enigmas abound. Is one becoming ill? Should one follow a certain trend? Should one try and become that nebulous entity of an "individual?" And here we have it. In a society of fluidity and diffuseness, where one can get irretrievably lost in a kaleidoscope of possible worlds, people often carve out what they wish to be an image of uniqueness—an identity constructed to keep at bay forces of uncertainty always threatening to assault them.

Now, the only setback with adopting the above tactic or *solution* is that most other people are doing exactly the same thing. So here it is again—the situation of the *free rider* problem. Just as one person feels that in taking a certain course of action it will be novel, even unique, it so happens that lots of other people are simultaneously pursuing the same strategy. Such psychological "clone-like" tactics may be used by people who never know or even see each other. The accumulation of such efforts is that people become further dissociated, are less absorbed into any sense of collectivity, distanced more and more from feelings of solidarity. Intimacy becomes more and more unlikely.

This trend towards greater social remoteness (distancing) was already seen to be in train by one of sociology's founding fathers, Emile Durkheim. He documented such work in his book *The Division of Labour*. Like Tonnies, he was especially interested in integration, and what he regrettably witnessed—a scene of receding social solidarity. He meant by this a reduction in human bonding or cohesiveness, a drifting away from fixed ties, a rootlessness, the backdrop of causation being industrial society. It was not just economic specialization; his division of labour concept permeated deep into the social fabric to include all institutions generally. Brilliantly, Durkheim's solution lay not in a return to an idyllic pre-industrial past for he saw this as both impossible as well as undesirable. For example, Durkheim saw religion as practised for millennia as totally inappropriate in a modern society. Instead, he advocated "occupational associations," that is, guilds in industry to reconcile conflicts. Behind such arrangements lay more fundamental recommendations by Durkheim such as an end to privilege, an end to the passing on of vast inheritance sums; in short, an attempt to severely reduce social and economic inequality. It was not so much that Durkheim saw inequality as unfair or unjust, but rather he saw it as constituting a spanner in the works of a better, smoother functioning social order. Only with a more equalitarian system would conflicts be reduced, and a lessening of an egoistic, selfish insularity.

Clearly Durkheim must be turning in his grave. The reason his vision has in no way materialized is no doubt due to the formidable difficulties not simply in achieving a more humane society, but in even trying to secure a modicum of consent in popular debate over what terms like equality or fairness even mean. This is perhaps harder to achieve currently than at any previous time. It is not due to a shortage of ability in those who could intelligently debate. Nor is it a case of insufficient factual data about poverty or who the rich and powerful might be. Rather, the kernel of the problem is that it may well be the case that even a modest attempt at a more humane and equal society will remain an unattainable goal so long as human life lasts. That is, a much wished-for dream, never to actually occur practically. Even were it a possibility, it is almost inconceivable at present given the ethos prevalent in polity and economy of the "right of the individual." So long as the "I'm all right, Jack" attitude prevails and is consciously and actively promoted and glorified, then any notions of community or consensus are extremely remote. Such matters as this individualistic ethos will be explored later, but here is the place to perhaps appropriately re-introduce a theme the previous arguments appear to have alluded to—the nature of mental illness and how it ties in with the above rather dry analysis.

As perhaps a plea for mitigation it can be said here that the preceding few pages deliberately skirted the mentally ill, both to avoid over complicating the discussions as well as to inject some crucial sociological theory on its own. This has the advantage of setting the scene into which our main theme can soon be inserted. We have by now constructed a sizeable enough roof to encompass a lot of influences upon mental health, loosely called "environmental" ones. More exactly, we have concentrated upon predispositional factors, those non-organic, endogenous influences which may act upon a hereditary base, be it vulnerable to such influences or not.

Summing up, we have looked in detail at social change, seeing it as a key element in psychological destabilization. More succinctly, we have tried to ascertain that the real factor operative is not simply "social change" but rather the *nature* of such change—its *pace*, its *intensity*. Having looked at such things, we now need to sharpen up a good deal on the much used woolly phrase of "organic base." Just what this is and the select few who are seemingly qualified to understand and deal with it (as a specialized discipline) is now the object of our enquiry.

Chapter 6

The Madness Mongers

Is there something endemic to the human condition to compel from birth (or even whilst still in the womb) some of us to a life of depressing derangement? Again, is there something endlessly elusive as to the cause (which we cannot even seem to identify) to, for lack of a better phrase, "put things right?" The actors in the scene are always present; we can see them. Either we pity them or ridicule them as they stand helplessly, pathetically in the spotlights. They are the mad. The stage is set; we await in feverish anticipation for some kind of action, some kind of remedy. This thin ray of hope exists despite the frustrating feeling we possess of defeatism that a cure could be as distant as the alchemist's dream of turning all metals into glittering gold. We nonetheless await very patiently, quite absorbed in something we don't really pretend to understand. Now the curtain is raised...suddenly they appear, centre stage...sombre, restrained but with an air of formidable power: The doctors. They are the stars in a long-lived epic, tragic tearjerker of great consistency and of worldwide dimension. Now we see them, we wonder, our mouths agape in dumbstruck awe. They tower over our minuscule knowledge on a subject we are simply just not qualified to even barely discuss. But they are qualified, they know. They. Enter the heroes and heroines: The madness mongers.

Often passing in everyday common parlance under such dubiously derogatory names as "shrinks" or "quacks," psychiatrists tend to be an undeservedly targeted breed. Either the popular press in sensationalized reportage forever fitting into a cliched formula give an incorrect impression that the doctors themselves are eccentric or too soft concerning their views of the insane criminal, or the man in the street views them with suspicion. Why, we might ask? The reason probably is simply rooted in our basic ignorance of the whole field of what psychiatrists claim to be their own highly specialized area of enquiry. As there is little if any attempt to break the ice in this lack of familiarity, the stalemate of ignorance simply persists. It may even be said that the public actually don't want, don't desire to know, regardless of whether they possess the capacity to understand psychiatric matters or not. They often feel irritatingly intimidated by them: The public see doctors on television, listen to them on Radio Three, and feel that all psychiatry is merely cloud cuckoo land. Unintelligible. So that often and quite unfairly psychiatrists are incorrectly dismissed as hare brained academic gurus who worship only their own useless textbooks, being superfluous to society; all of them get tarred with this same brush that also gets so oversweepingly applied to social workers, psychologists, or community workers—that is, those professions that prefer to avoid the accounts of daily tabloids and actually try to ascertain useful information about the mentally ill and try to help them.

Once again, rather than to even try to understand the issues involved, the public tend to put up blinds of disdain founded upon their ignorance. Perhaps the reason for this is also that the actual field of social or "people" work, because of its very intangibility (lack of any visible product), leads many of us to assume that psychiatric output is worthless. Whereas the businessman can state that 100,000 automobiles were produced by his company the other month and are now available for public purchase in attractive, brightly lit showrooms, the psychiatrist can only "produce" words or statements about what his/her contribution to "production" has been. This output, due to its very invisibility or lack of physical material form, is further exacerbated by the quite ambiguous content of the psychiatrists' workload and throughout. The impression often fostered by mass media agencies and eagerly absorbed by the public of "people work" (as being non-productive) is both false and unfair.

Such misplaced views have always been the case of the social science professions, and even of the arts. The public tend to think of a contribution to net wealth or happiness only by means of actual physical production. Talk, debates, arguments, seminars, discussions—so very much a part of a discipline such as mental health—are assumed to be just hot air. Just a waste of time, useless, even counter-productive sometimes in that they are felt to be a brake on *real* producers who actually "make something" which we can drive, wear, or eat. Thus, a dearth of material consumability gives rise to an unfortunate array of incorrectly conceived stereotypes of doctors. The doctors are seen to be managers who are incompetent in dealing with the equally misunderstood group in society—the mad.

This particular series of stereotypes has little altered over a long period of time. This is mainly for the reason that the majority of the public are not particularly interested, don't understand the matters involved and, most importantly, it is not in the public's interest to push for policies which would in any way enhance their understanding. For as long as the automobile production line keeps churning out nicely sparkling cars, architects keep drawing up imaginative designs for new homes, and the latest fashion experts give us yet new novelties in our attire, then who really bothers about the mad, and the managers of the mad? Who really cares? The matter of who exactly does care will be our point of discussion later on, but here we will explore the possibility of insanity having its roots in heredity. Coupled with this is the ammunition devised so far to effect a "cure," interwoven with a welter of unforeseen problems and conflicts within the mental health sphere itself.

It frequently is the case that practitioners of disciplines encounter difficulty in trying, when asked, to actually define their discipline. It is not so much an effort to try and specify the content of the job or what they do, but rather to sum up in a neat, unambiguous sentence what they are trying to achieve or ultimately contribute to notions of welfare or progress in society. Nowhere is this more notoriously the case than in mental health. It is highly questionable whether or not there is any adequate understanding, let alone precise definition, of what the human mind actually is, what its purpose is, how exactly it functions. The enormous intricacy—from which there radiate so many different aspects begging for an accurate analysis—behaviour, emotions, aggressive traits, or passive traits, to name just a few properties of the brain. And, of course, this is compounded (this embryonic knowledge) when we switch to abnormal thinking promoting deviant actions, that is forensic psychiatry. Even very basic problems raise themselves, ones of a slightly moral or philosophical kind, such as to try and elucidate distinctions between normality and abnormality. When is violent behaviour acceptable or unacceptable; in what context? Do leaders in national military conflicts come under the same medical scrutiny of possessing aggressive pathology as the offender who commits homicide during peacetime?

Such modes of relativisation are a useful way of introducing some flexibility into our study, revealing philosophical, ethical dilemmas, but it also has its snags. Principally, using too much speculation and rationalization can frustratingly trap us in an endless circle of unresolved relativism. This is the heart of the blockage, the impasse confronting social scientists at the present time; that is, moral relativization, the should's, should not's, why's, why not's of subjective types of professions—a key one being psychiatric work. So, which way out of the snakepit?

What could perhaps here push forward the frontiers of this debate so long stuck in confusion is to try and keep out, eliminate the unanswerable moral side of ethics, at least in the early stages of our study. This is very helpful, particularly if we also avoid chronological relativism and comparison; that is, to concentrate solely on the here and now. Otherwise, the whole effort is scurried with clouds of confusion and will proceed nowhere. Still, the mention of philosophy concerning psychiatric practice was not wholly without benefit. It made a good point, namely that the social world is not a neutral, blank collection of people; rather those people, those social actors have different interests, different resources and power, and for these exact reasons, ethicality is perpetually present whenever we study social behaviour and organization of it. The field of mental health is no rose garden of immortal perfection and unanimous consensus; it is fraught with conflict and this is why, if we are to try and conduct a useful study, ethics of psychiatric practice must be firmly understood to exist, to be the foundations of our enquiry—even if we omit them at times to simplify our analytic method of procedure.

The above views have a familiar resonance with previous chapters— the matter of power, interests, and upsetting of applecarts; of common sense, comfortably established conventional wisdom. In a way this is perfectly understandable—many of us resent social scientists bombarding us with loads of questions—for we all feel entitled to our own private thoughts, being perturbed by quizzing investigations. Yet only by understanding one another's content of thought, especially that thought felt to be private or personal, will any genuinely useful knowledge ever be gained about, to use a somewhat woolly term, the human psyche. And this is the big paradox: People avidly pay lip service to adventurous enterprises ostensibly in business to widen human understanding. This could be so in attempts to cure cancer and AIDS, control pollution, reduce overpopulation, create a "fairer" society, prevent Third World starvation, and also prevent the plight of mental illness. But in order that such kinds of problems might be tackled or even approached, researchers need to know more about people's lifestyles, cultures, modes of thought. And clearly, such an ambitious endeavour clashes with people's sense of privacy and the basic right to be able to go about their lives peacefully without being the guinea pigs of people seen as nosey, inconsiderate researchers.

This neatly ties in with the ethos of the psychiatric knowledge, which is still quite rudimentary and can only increase by doctors asking people basic but valuable questions such as what they like, hate, what they would like to have done, why, or whatever; then the analysis could get a little sharper, deeper, and start to ask whether or not some people possess unreal expectations, get things out of perspective, have negative views of themselves (a bad self-image). Such types of questions have a very personal character; those being asked are parting with quite confidential information about themselves which many prefer not to divulge. So here then, the upshot for the doctor is that it is a massive uphill struggle in learning much (particularly new) that is what has not already been in the standard textbooks ad nauseam. More to the point, in clinical psychiatry (of deviations from some apparent norm) it leaves us in a poor situation of not knowing alternative kinds of possible norm—possessed by deviants who do not subscribe to the official mainstream norm, who genuinely feel and believe and act in a manner otherwise; that is a different kind of normality, a possession of a different type of conscience, a different scale of values. Only by listening to lots of different human beings can a useful assessment be made about what is and what is not regarded as normal, just, fair, unfair, good, or bad. Any heavy, highbrow philosophy need not enter into it. Simply everyday life in everyday society as experienced and perceived by everyday people will do the job of analysis excellently. Much is to be said for an empirical approach, especially one that avoids unnecessarily smuggling in heavy doses of philosophy. Indeed, this infiltration of ethics by cool, detached researchers is exactly the cause of so much confusion to date. It is not that the problems are simple to solve, but that the methodology required to try and solve them can be relatively simple. Complex research designs, it seems (and is now widely agreed), have been the ball and chain of clarity and comprehension in social services.

It is no secret that the typical tool kit of the contemporary psychiatrist consists a great deal of learning from existing material in the profession, such as reading literature on case histories, or papers upon more biological topics such as glands or chemicals in the brain; how these affect behaviour, how this might be modified by chemotherapy. Also, and not to be straight-away belittled, is a lot of information derived from work on animals, seen to be of relevance to understanding some aspects of humans, such as work done on chimpanzees or rats.

It is at this point that we can expand upon our subject's actual range of practitioners; for increasingly madness mongers are no longer just psychiatrists. Crucially there are also clinical psychologists. What puzzles many people is the difference between them. Well, is there any? Certainly there exists a dissimilar focus, despite the fact that the overall thrust of enquiry is the same and a recognition mutually of a broadly shared subject matter— mentally ill people. This is not just glib rhetoric, for many patients are often very distressed, disillusioned people who need confidence instilled in them. They require help (such as the need to develop insight) precisely because the debilitating nature of their condition prevents them acquiring such faculties endogenously. If it cannot come from within (that is, self-aware-ness), then it has to come from an external source—hence, the supposed rationale for the entire psychiatric apparatus which has developed both through philanthropic motives plus an unavoidably emergent necessity.

Yet whereas a psychiatrist is interested in instilling considerable faith in biological intervention such as drugs, electric shock treatment, or even psychosurgery, the psychologist is especially keen on identifying the social or environmental influences. These may, for example, be such factors as parental or peer group pressures and relationships, or issues such as self-image, isolation, frustration. Often attitudes of such states are seen by psychologists to be a direct result of having been in a psychiatric institu-tion—artificial places hardly conducive to developing skill flexibility as is increasingly required in a highly fluid, changeable modern world. So the psychiatrists' actual perspective is almost as if to be looking for a kind of disease of the mind, a chemical imbalance to be appropriately remedied by physical intervention such as medication. But this procedure of treatment should not be derided as pure bunkum. For often, when a patient is profoundly disturbed and unable to calm down and relax through counsel-ling, drug treatment may be the only option left. This is a very crucial point. For so often critics unfairly jibe doctors whom they see as obsessional about prescribing medication. It has to be said here that as there is yet still no outright miracle cure available, it boils down to having to do the best with what limited techniques of treatment currently exist.

And yet this is not to wholly side with the psychiatrists either. For there is abundant evidence that often such interventions clumsily called "treat-ment" (such as drug prescribing or electric shocks) have been quite indis-criminately and disgracefully dished out to patients for several decades. Many such patients had no option whatsoever but to have to be put through a minefield of so-called therapies, each particular therapy constituting a mine which exploded with damaging effects upon their bodies. It could be senile dementia through drugs taken over many years or permanent loss of memory from E.C.T. sessions. Either way, patients until very recently had no say in the matter, never being consulted for their consent to a battery of often hit or miss, even largely useless "therapy."

It is at this point where the psychologist comes in as a useful counter-force to such a monopoly as consultant psychiatrists possess as regards authority in deciding patients' treatment programmes. For the psychologist often points out that a disturbed patient may well not require any medicine at all (and here would be at loggerheads with the psychiatrist). But the psychologist may go yet further, stating that the entire problem the patient is seen as suffering from is not in the least bit the patient's actual fault. It may be argued that the patient who is seen as "abnormally neurotic" suffered severe beatings as a child by his or her parents, and has never got over it. That is, past history could alter the present facts of the matter considerably, and help to repaint the picture—a different picture from that embraced by the psychiatrist. Here the psychologist is clearly saying that the patient was not born mentally ill, was not even predisposed to becoming so; instead was forced by virtue of circumstance to have to undergo cruelty and neglect. From this the psychological perspective deduces that the process of early socialization for preparing the patient for the world of adulthood or late adolescence was tragically faulty. Hence the current (supposedly inadequate) neurosis is not in the least bit organically derived, nor the patient's own personality deficiency either. As regards treatment, it is not so much drug therapy that is needed any more (and should henceforth be discontinued) but an in-depth programme of sensitive counselling as a kind of adult skills of coping rehabilitation. In this way, needless incarceration could have or can be avoided in a mental hospital as well as the stupefying side effects of unnecessary drugs. Social skills can be acquired instead, life skills to last a literal lifetime, and not short term palliatives of medication as the psychiatrist erroneously thought suitable.

Indeed, the whole issue of psychiatric incarceration will be looked at in the next chapter, and the question of decarceration (that is not locking people up) will be evaluated as to whether it is both a more effective as well as humane response. Provocatively, it will be seen that when we take on board the situation of the patient who has offended, that has committed a criminal offence, it raises a lot of problems for our discussion. However, we can here lay some fertile ground for the chapter following this which looks at forensic psychiatry. This can here be done by studying the types of mental abnormality of the criminal patient; this tidily returns us to very real problems encountered by the psychiatrist. This area is red hot with controversy, it is a critical site of difficult decision making for any consultant. An exact diagnosis has to be made on just what it is that the patient is actually suffering from. It is an area of unresolved opinion for, after all, if defining normal is a perplexing exercise, then abnormal is even more so. Yet the media, public, and legal bodies continually clamour for watertight, specific facts, details, and an indisputable medical diagnostic determination which unenviably lies entirely in the doctor's lap.

It is not clear that the main lines of disagreement and criticism focus on the diagnostic procedure. This is very important. It will affect not only the doctor's reputation (should diagnosis turn out to be wrong) but also it will affect, to a large extent, the future of the patient. Such a cost for the patient's future could be measured in length of stay in an institution, but more insidious things will also inevitably creep in—hence, the actual treatment procedure and autonomy in society, the kind of restrictions placed upon a patient over a long period of time, maybe for life.

Now we are drawn towards the real nitty gritty at the centre of forensic medical work—classification of offenders. Without a risk of overgenerali-zation, here it could be said that the two major categories which arouse most controversy are those of schizophrenia and psychopathology. Just which label is applied is the source of the conflict. Such antagonisms rage not only between doctors themselves, but between doctor and judge, doctor and prosecution counsel, doctor and patient, doctor and patient's relatives, doctor and media, doctor and the Department of Health. Even more intense is, as we shall see in the following two chapters, the conflict between doctors and the major gatekeepers in forensic matters—the home office personnel. There is a very good reason why there is so much argument, loss of reputations, public scandal, cover ups, legal embarrassments, about the chance of an incorrect diagnostic procedure surrounding schizophrenia or psychopathy. Let us look at this problem facing the consultant taking discrepant interests into account.

The problem arises because there is a lot of disagreement amongst medical experts themselves as to whether psychopathy is a mental illness or not. As far as most of the general public are concerned, the word psychopath is synonymous with Hitchcock's "Psycho." That is a cold-blooded, calculating maniac who, once caught should be placed securely behind bars forever, or even better, should have been put down at birth. In the public's eyes the psychopath is not mad, but bad, a rotten apple. A closely related view is that psychopaths are incurable social misfits that nobody can do anything with, are unsuitable and unworthy of assistance, especially financed out of taxpayer's money. They therefore should either be jailed for natural life or be taken out in a quiet field and shot. Most certainly, the psychopath is assumed by many to be inhuman, lustful, impulsively and uncontrollably volatile, something society can well do without. Such a hot plate of qualms, worries, and prejudiced stereotypes all falls onto the doctors' place at the table. They have the tough task of sticking to their canons of professional clinical judgement and also impossibly satisfying lots of other parties involved in a case. As for the public's attitude, this requires little imagination as to what should be done to the patient; that is, the view is a retributive, often vindictive one of "an eye for an eye" nature. For the public desire invariably a punitive outcome rather than a therapeutic one; that is, to avoid being "too soft" with the patient.

On the other hand, there is the plight of the actual patient who may be in a terrible state of mental turmoil, not even aware of what is going on. Memory of recent events may be severely impaired, such a state of amnesia being brought on by shock or a crushing bout of depression. Equally, their minds may be full of terrifying delusions, or the thought that they are being conspired against, that nobody is their friend anymore. There may be hallucinatory states such as voices from Satan, telling the patient to do all sorts of horrible things, or there may be simply a splintering up of everyday life into a chaotic, confusing meaninglessness—where nothing can be ascertained to be real anymore. And it is important to understand this—that delusional or hallucinatory states are just and every bit as real to the Schizophrenic as every day events are to a person not so afflicted.

For mental illness is not an intermittently visited fantasy world, like an odd outing to a frenetic, dizzy fairground. No. Rather, insanity is most truly a whole world, a total existence. It absorbs the sufferer's entire vision, the entire thought process. Its unreality is as real to the patient as reality is real to somebody who is regarded as perfectly sane. It is exactly for reasons connected with the above incapacitating states of mind that diagnoses must be highly accurate. The whole problem revolves around whether the offender concerned is schizophrenic or more inclined towards psychopathy. This is because the relative state of mental incapacitation is usually greater for the schizophrenic at the exact time of committing his or her legal transgression. It follows from this that the schizophrenic is accorded a larger amount of sympathy; that is, is seen as having a better "excuse" for having broken the law. This sympathy is very meager for the psychopathic offender. What the psychiatrist is specifically looking for is psychotic behaviour, which is usually absent in psychopathy but widespread for a schizophrenic type of condition. For a psychosis is generally considered to remove conscious volition, rendering a state of irresponsibility. But the psychopath, in not being psychotic, is assumed to quite knowingly, with conscience faculties intact (despite being somewhat disordered), have gone out onto the streets and blatantly and deliberately offended.

From this all kinds of symptoms are attached to psychopaths, such as emotional superficiality, inadequacy, poor socialites, dominant, manipulators to name but a few traits widely recognized by doctors. It can get even more emotive than this. Some doctors see in psychopaths a ruthless desperation of hedonistic impulsiveness, the desire to win at all costs, regardless of having inflicted pain or misery upon others.

Bad news for the budding psychopath? It all seems as if the odds are against anyone being classed as such. This was certainly so until only very recently. Now, although it is still by no means an agreed thing by all doctors, the balance has to an extent been redressed. Psychopaths are getting a little (but it is only a little) more understanding from doctors, although the public intransigence is well nigh unchanged. The altering of the balance is a result of a lot of hard work in clinical research which has quite convincingly shown that psychopathy in certain forms (but not all forms) can be classed as a mental illness proper—as debilitating as a schizophrenic psychotic phase in impairing rational thought.

Many psychopaths have had a totally abnormal childhood with a massively distorted, ruptured upbringing. Their formative years may have been ones of receiving little or no love from parents (and in some cases no parentage anyway, instead an orphanage). In a complicated way, they many have as a necessary survival (sink or swim) tactic, had to develop anti-social or deviant ways of coping, of handling life. Such maladaptive behaviour being to them acceptable, or just the only way open to solve social problems, the acceptable skills used by normal people having never been acquired, due to an abnormal infant development. Furthermore, and in stark opposition to the conventional folklore, it has been found that the actual targets for a psychopath's inadequacy and insecurity are not other people at all, but themselves. Be it self-inflicted slashes from razor blades or attempted (even successful) suicidal behaviour, their frustration engendered by a self-awareness of their social incompleteness is a serious clinical problem. Self-mutilation is a cry for help which a society, ostensibly a caring one, should at least recognize as a glaring fact. Obviously, if a human being possesses such a sense of dehumanizing despair, of hopelessness, as many psychopaths most surely do, then it cannot be lightly dismissed as a mere, superficial neurosis.

So much is this the case that anybody unacquainted with actual individual cases (as opposed to media-hype sensationalized constructions) who states that psychopaths should be punished, is exhibiting psychopathy themselves—in its most vicious manifestations. Attitudes of public hostility and dearth of empathy are in fact often projections, that is negative feelings vented by the public onto psychopaths, in an effort by the public to (falsely) reassure themselves as sane and impeccably law abiding.

Such contradictions in our morality abound. They have above been easily seen in our evaluation of different types of clinical diagnosis to fit different types of legal offenders. This is why diagnosis is crucial. It will affect the length of stay of a patient; the schizophrenic may serve three years, the psychopath thirty, for exactly the same offence. The different length of sentences for each offender is due to stereotypical myths of what a psychopath is, such as a monster or beast.

All of the above arguments have hopefully shown just what an imprecise, hazy business psychiatry is. Much is still unclear and misunderstood. Also, psychiatrists are only human, fallible beings like everybody else. This is the source of the pressure. The public expect them to be infallible, superhuman, never wrong. And when they are wrong, all hell is heaped upon them. Such unjust criticisms are and can only continue to be counterweights to advance in the clinical field, millstones around attempts to further understand the plight of the mentally ill, who themselves are victims and, invariably, undeservedly so.

This being the current scenario we can see that punishing the ill deviant puts us back into a distant draconian age which cannot be in any way able to state that it is humanitarian. For it is surely a contradiction in terms to give human beings their just desserts when they totally believed that at the time of offending they were agents of God or Satan. That is, they were acting in a delusional capacity, being utterly devoid of rational, reasonable cognition. They may also retain such delusions till the day they die. We are often told, though we do not like to accept it, it is often only when we ourselves contract an often quite unpredictable mental malaise that we realize our own infallibility. A world most surely spinning around in a normal, taken-for-granted fashion, can suddenly start throwing people off into orbits of abnormality.

Chapter 7

False Sense of Security

Just as many people who feel uneasy about psychiatry prefer such a matter out of sight (that is, are reluctant to confront it), so the actual locations for managing the mad are equally well out of vision. For whereas factories, foundries, mills, offices, streets, housing estates, shops, and especially entertainment facilities are almost always in our gaze, this is not so often the case for those who have been selectively siphoned off from mainstream society. Indeed, it is uncommon for urban, built-up areas to contain psychiatric locations. Either they occupy small wings of massive general hospitals or are situated well out on the periphery of towns, but even this is to speak only of the minority of mental hospitals. For the vast bulk of them occupy the most rural of settings. This has two very basic implications—firstly, the public can invariably go about their day-to-day lives without hardly ever crossing paths with a patient and, secondly, a patient hardly ever (during the respective period of confinement) enters the actual space of everyday social interaction.

Usually the view from a patient's bedroom window is not of skyscrapers and busy streets jammed with traffic. Instead, it is a rolling undulation of countryside, hills, a river perhaps; above all, just field after field receding into what must be a curiously contemplated horizon. This is what most patients see; such a scene is their panorama for twelve months or thirty years, sometimes even longer. It may be all they will ever see for the rest of their days. So much for sight. As for sound, what a patient hears is not a tooting of car horns, cafeteria conversation, or vans of loudspeakers broadcasting electioneering slogans. Rather, it is the sounds of cows, sheep, and combine harvesters now and then. Also, the never-ending jangling of keys turning in doors and unvarying shouts of "breakfast , dinner up, tea up, supper up, medications, bed up." So that to use their original name, asylums are dotted up and down the country (of which there are a great amount);

invariably in the middle of nowhere. It is most truly a situation of the "out of sight, out of mind." The reasons for this may either be separate or there may be interlinked competing explanations. The most superficial reason usually invoked is that to locate a hospital in the middle of Berkshire (as Broadmoor was in 1863), has the advantage of letting the inmates have access to fresh air amidst what is beautiful country scenery. This would certainly appear better than a location amidst an urban jungle. This is a quite valid point. On the other tack it could be said that mental hospitals and their respective locations have, behind their planning, construction, and ultimate geographical setting, got a rationale very much akin to prisons.

For if hospitals are well out of the way of the general public, then obviously most people do not have to see them, recognize them, accept them with any responsibility, guilt or doubt or fear. After all, who really wants a prison full of criminals just a hundred yards down the road from one's house? There might be an escape of a convict who might take a hostage—it could be you or me. It is not so much the unsightliness of a prison itself which is at the root of the public's qualms (even though most prisons *are* unsightly). It is rather an irrational, continuously nagging uncertainty for the public about "bad people" being close to one's particular haven; a bit too close for comfort.

Indeed, we see this borne out in practice: Peterhead in remote rural Scotland, Gartree in the remote Midlands, Parkhurst on the Isle of Wight, or Dartmoor amidst the mists and mire of Devonshire. Such is also the case with mental hospitals. For the five (no more) maximum security units in Britain, Cartstairs is in the heart of Lanarkshire countryside, Broadmoor equally isolated in Berkshire, Rampton lost in the rolling fields of Nottinghamshire, and the twin Ashworth complex on the outer fringes of Merseyside. So much for the high security or special hospital sites. But there are many less secure hospitals, often called locals, and, since the early 1980s, an emergence of what are referred to as Regional Secure Units, also having very "out of the way" peripheral locations. All share one common feature: They are on the outer limits of mainstream social activity. Now, for a society which professes to show concern and interest in the plight of the less fortunate, such a marginalization clearly represents yet another contradiction, inasmuch as I care, you care, we all care, but would much prefer it if *somebody else* did the actual caring.

The last comment brings us to the more subjective side of it all; the matter, for instance, of just what mechanisms are involved in the decision making of who decides (and why) about where people actually get sent. This can be a highly sensitive, debatable issue, encompassing lots of disagreement. For this is the battlefield of criminal pathology. Forensic Psychiatry clearly deals not simply with people who happen to be mentally disordered, for a legal infraction has also taken place. The type of actual offence is an important factor to take into account as its relative seriousness will most definitely affect the type of hospital to which the patient is sent. The more trivial (and more often committed) offenses such as theft or breaches of the peace usually implies a very short period in a low security, local hospital. However, if it is the respective consultant's view that the patient who, despite being only a petty offender, warrants a long stay due to a psychiatric problem of perceived severity, then a minor lawbreaker could spend ten years inside a mental hospital, albeit of minimal security. The freedom is still effectively thus denied—here on purely clinical grounds—more specifically on the personal opinions of somebody with enormous power—a psychiatrist. Such a state of affairs can lead us to see that it can be very difficult to draw a clear conclusion concerning severity of offence and length of custodial placement in psychiatric cases. Further-more, here anomalies abound, for often very serious offenders spend only a relatively short time in mental hospitals, whereas a very petty but very sick offender could be put away for life.

Much has to do with the initial interview on remand in prison; that is, between prisoner and consultant in the hospital wing. A great deal hinges upon this initial series of discussions. If the doctor feels unable to discern any immediate signs of dangerousness, then providing the index offence has not been notably newsworthy, a place such as a top security hospital will not be the place the inmate will go to. Broadmoor has been mentioned as it is fairly familiar with the public, as for that matter is now Rampton or Ashworth. These semi-mysterious maximum security units are a very important part of the psychiatric criminal justice system. They affect many different people, permeate deep into emotive public debates, although in the end the net impact will be shouldered by the patient. It might therefore be interesting to look a little more closely here at these special, high security institutions, paying attention to types of offender, types of offence actually committed and, critically, what determines the length of incarceration.

It might be supposed that the mental state of the patient was the sole determining factor, but as our analysis proceeds it will be shown that this is by no means always correct. Primarily, when the defendant is brought to trial in crown court (although this does not always warrant a jury proceeding), most of the debate will revolve around the "mad or bad" problem. But during the period of remand this will usually already have been decided through the compilation and submission, to the prosecution, of medical reports. Hence, although it seems virtually certain that the defendant will be placed on a hospital order, it is not quite so certain which level of security is required. The jury, but most importantly the judge and prosecution counsel, will have a great deal of influence in this. Even more subtly, the actual sensitivity of the case will influence the prosecution's recommendations. For undoubtedly a great splash of publicity around the time of the offenses and appearance of offender at Crown Court (that is, all the pre-trial build up of hype and public interest and reaction) certainly helps to sway the outcome.

All the publicity build up is no doubt loathed, not least by the defence counsel, for it exerts a kind of pressure which says: "Severely deal with this offender who has committed a severe legal transgression." Hence, if the offence and case generally had *not* attracted a lot of media coverage, then even the homicidal (even multiple homicidal) offender could be quietly processed through the criminal/medical apparatus. The patient-soon-to-be could perhaps be sent to a regional secure unit, instead of a high security or special hospital. But if the case had been one to really hit the headlines, such as one striking deep into the outrage of the public, then the security level to be sent to will be of a maximum. Much depends on the nature of the actual crime. By "nature" it is meant the emotive kind of response invoked in the public, such as their anger, hate even, of killers of children, serial killers, multiple rapists, or sadists. Equally, the law's reaction to certain types of crimes is important also—such as the murder of police officers or prison officers. All these have in common the potential to affect emotions, often clouding the facts; that is, people tend to react with a gut response of furious indignation. All of this is fuelled by a popular media system which thrives on sensationalized newsworthiness. So that when the day of the trial comes, there is a highly strung atmosphere of unmitigated, unwavering expectancy that there should be no grounds for leniency or sympathy for the offender in question. Justice must be seen to be done.

This set of ideas is quite fascinating—emotions clouding issues factual in content. For it is not in any way incorrect to argue the case that certain patients who are in special hospitals and have been there for twenty, even thirty years, still without a chance of release, are victims of this "sensitivity" syndrome. That is, their cases are red hot and nobody wishes to handle such hot potatoes. It is not so much that the public don't forget, but instead it is the mass media, in its endless quest for newsworthy topics, that will not allow an emotively charged crime (no matter how long ago) to settle into public forgetfulness. A case of twenty years ago can, if the tabloid's editorial staff so wish, be hyped up all over again, almost as if it had occurred only yesterday. It is in this way that the public are always aware of particular serious cases. Time is not always a good or effective healer. The media see to that. The public's memories are forever fuelled, jolted into remembrance of what a newspaper feels should be, and crime is a favourite topic.

This tight situation is especially tight for those who have been trying to keep the case "hush hush" since it initially arose and the perpetrator was put away. This quietening down is desired in the slim hope that the patient could be eased out of a special hospital to perhaps a hospital of lesser security without any hue and cry. The patient and relatives may also have attempted to keep things low profile, too; but needless to say, the press can destroy all such efforts.

So it is a convoluted issue, not simply a medical versus legal matter, but instead all kinds of competing parties who all vie with one another due to quite different standpoints. It is not thus just prosecution versus defence, or offender versus victim; it has repercussions of a far wider dimension.

Bearing such implications in mind, let us study a bit of the public's psychology here. Now, the public obviously do often react in emotive extremes, and yet it is a little more complicated in that these emotions are often substituted for facts. This has to be so; feelings are the bedrock of our very personalities, affect our responses and attitudes towards other people. It is how people actually feel about something—say something to antagonise them which structures a reaction—but reactions, we can here see, are not always based upon factual events or concrete circumstances; they are affected by (often distorted) *perceptions*. There is often a massive difference between what is perceived and what has actually happened. It is often people's perceptions, fuelled by a distinctively emotive base, which dictates their responsiveness to an apparently purely factual matter.

Hence, if we take the plight of those classed as criminally insane, the public might (or might not) grant them a little sympathy, if not empathy, if the offence is thought to have been quite grave. This is the public's own *personal* opinion, a purely private, undisclosed one. But if asked, say by a media agency, and the statement made is to be publicly quoted for others to hear, then the opinion given will often be a middle-of-the-road, conventional one, to appease potential critics with oppositional views. Hence, "hang them, birch them, jail them for life" responses are typical general public utterances when asked to pronounce opinions on psychiatric offenders. What little sympathy as does exist is swamped by the safe impulse to go along with a conventional mainstream morality.

And yet it is still superficial to just leave our analysis at that. It goes much deeper. For why should the public wish to continue to condemn ill offenders to years and years of damaging, stultifying incarceration? Many reasons, some already touched upon, are responsible. A major one is that people can only identify or put themselves in the shoes of somebody else if they know all the circumstances of an offence. But it takes much more than simply that. For crucially, they would need to know (which they never can or ever will) what the offender went through mentally. That is, how the mind was deteriorating over a period of time until it finally disintegrated, taking powers of reason, judgement, volition, and conscience generally with it. There is a well known adage that nobody knows exactly how another person feels; that is, to actually sense somebody else's emotion, their intensity, or richness. Now, one can obviously feel sorry for somebody who is in a bad way and feel sympathetic, but that is only identifying with somebody else's experience; it is not feeling it, living it.

Bearing this in consideration, it follows that actions *not yet committed* (that is, never having been experienced) personally, by somebody effectively negates their capacity for empathy for anybody else *who has* undergone such an experience. This means an incomplete ability to fully identify, to understand motivation and temperament which the actual offender went through at the time of committing the crime. This rules out a state of reasonableness in the content of any arguments marshalled against the offender, such arguments as might be voiced by an indignant, morally incensed public. Such emotional reactions as they do occur are thus tainted, not so much with any predetermined element of bias, but inadequate familiarization.

But this is to portray an unfair appraisal of the public's mental powers; for it is not the public and the public alone who arrive at an unfair caricature of offenders. There is a mischievous intermediary—the popular press. For the public do not normally or frequently act or react hysterically or in an unbalanced way. Hysterical emotions don't often surface, they only tend to surface for hysterical, unnatural situations. Such situations are induced by unnatural, hysterical accounts; that is, sensationalized data provided by the popular media. So it is not inherent in the public psyche to possess a draconian, retributive propensity; to say, unequivocally and impulsively, "hang them, flog them, jail them." That is, the public do not independently, of their own respective powers of judgement, arrive at remorseless, grim condemnations of offenders; only by the infiltration into their consciousness, of a misleading account of criminality by the media, does such a state of affairs arise.

So that most people are *made to react* through the actual content of the information presented to them—in many cases by the popular public conscience—our daily newspaper. Sticking to the train of this reasoning procedure is to say that a human being regards or is made to regard, to visualize, that is to perceive a seemingly unnatural act of behaviour as the act of one who is inhuman, a totally different kind of being. For example, a killer of children is perceived by many of the population as absolutely inhuman. This is because most of the population have been continuously culturally conditioned, moulded throughout their entire lives, to treat such an offence with anathema. They have not had the genetic (or cultural) mishap (or disturbance within their brains) to precipitate committing or even contemplating committing such an offence themselves; that is, personally. Since childhood, such non-offenders have every little piece of their socialization learned such an offence to be not human, or comprehensible. Such an offender is thus "not one of us, not one of our kind."

This is exacerbated by the labels the press give to the offender, serving to further corroborate such fixed, unchanging mental pictures. Such derogatory levels also hype up and infamously glorify such images, so that we come to expect a killer to actually *look* different; a twisted face, foaming at the mouth, bulging eyes, and so forth—"Fiends," "beasts," and "maniacs" (as the press refer to insane criminals) we expect to actually look the part, look unlike *normal* people.

Such stereotypes based on misperceptions serve to put the offenders where it is felt they truly should belong—*not* in a mental hospital or a prison even, but in *another world*—a place like hell, for those perceived to be unnatural, inhuman, uncivilized, who do not belong to humanity any more. Another planet perhaps; then the offender will most truly be alienated. This relegation to a marginal location in society has in the past been taken even further; the insane offender has at the time of the death penalty been literally sent to somewhere which nobody alive could understand or explain—to death, and that existence or plane which encompasses lifelessness after this world. That is, the execution of offenders constitutes marginalization par excellence. The philosophy of forensic psychiatry invites interesting speculation, if readily much needed substantive suggestions, for implementation into hard policy. So let us return to our chain of process in the system and how it affects the offender. After the court appearance, a prison sentence having been deemed inappropriate, it has been stated that a bed is waiting at a special hospital; the length of confinement being without any fixed limit, that is it is for an indefinite period. What this term "indefinite" actually turns out to be in practice, we might wonder? The answer is it could be a few months or a lifetime. This hazy but ominous possibility is the brooding storm cloud hanging over what appears to be a pleasant stay in hospital—quiet, restful, pleasant stay in hospital, a quiet restful sanctuary for inmates. This is rarely, if ever, the rose garden of special hospital nitty gritty reality.

On admission to a special hospital it is noticed that the actual buildings and layout are very different from a local hospital; that is, one of low security. A special hospital has a high perimeter wall, well nigh unclimbable; the doors all have locks and most windows have bars. Somewhere our new admission will be housed, routine tests will be done—such as a physical examination, blood tests, a visit to the dentist—and a kit of standard hospital clothing may be given out, the same colour and kind of dress worn by maybe 500 other patients there.

Depending upon both mental state and what the doctor and staff see as suitable progress, the length of stay for the patient may be roughly (but only roughly) gauged. But what exactly is progress and, more exactly, what does progress mean to a psychiatrist? Generally it implies such changes in the patient's mental state such as greater stability, lack of adverse reports (such as being cooperative, not aggressive or threatening), complying with hospital or ward policy. But these are the more obvious indications. More profound signs of what constitutes improvement tend to be less tangible (although very important) in overall progress evaluation; things like moods, tolerance, reasonableness, rationality, lucidity in thought—all over a period of time under a lot of intensive observation.

In the succeeding chapter we will carry on from these signs of apparent progress to critically question the actual length of time it is sensible or reasonable in which to expect them to become manifest. Many critics feel the time is far too excessive, that release dates should and could occur far sooner than is currently so. That is, that benefits from what treatments a special hospital provides are exhausted but patients still remain confined there, a situation analogous to serving life imprisonment. But this, it will be seen, is not by any means always the fault of doctors or staff but rather the matter we have looked at earlier—of the sensitivity of particular patient's cases in the media and public consciousness. That is the politics of forensic psychiatry.

Such a climate of moral sensitivity is not something essentially new on the scene; it has always been around. But in the specific British political and economic climate since the early 1970s, there has certainly emerged much more of a media and general public awareness (misperceived or not) based upon a political, electoral law and order platform. This has completely transformed people's views on forensic psychiatry, especially the mentally ill criminal. It can be said that such changes have independently created a context in which crime and mental illness have and continue to be the subject of far greater scrutiny by many different kinds of people and with this, corresponding views about appropriate deterrents to be dished out.

Such a recent emphasis upon deterrents is in no way connected with the nature of the offenses committed—extremely serious crimes have occurred throughout the centuries accompanied by insane perpetrators— never in previous human history has there been such an intense media interest in such cases. This has promoted a consequent public awareness; that is, the public have been forced to consider the criminally ill, what they have done wrong, and what should be done with them. This could typically be how long an indefinite period should, in reality, effectively mean.

It is precisely here that we see the seemingly neutral term "indefinite period" as no longer so innocently neutral or sacrosanctity removed from public influence. An indefinite period can be made to mean different things; that is, it can have a desired, implicit time configuration built into it by people who so desire this. It can and is now a highly flexible term whose innocent absence of temporality is coloured by human prejudice, as to what it should really mean.

In fact, for many patients the term indefinite period is a very misleading hope-booster. After admission to a special hospital, the reality of length of stay shows "indefinite" to be a somewhat meaningless (even rather useless) kind of phrase. In the contemporary British law and order climate, custodial criteria are both closer to the essence of the issue and cut through the woolly tangle of the whole procedure. It is invariably now a custodial situation confronting special hospital inmates; let us be in no doubt about that. For although the patients are getting treatment, they are (with every passing day) alsodoingtime. They are, just as the prisoner in jail, losing their liberty. And when it comes to recommendations by the clinical team for transfer to a less secure unit or outright discharge, the patient's case sensitivity usually means the recommendations fall on stoney ground and the patient simply clocks up more and more years in an institution which is no longer in any way useful as to treatment criteria. Instead, it is wrongful, implicit application of custodial criteria.

Whom then is blocking the patient's chances of getting out of special hsopitals? For if it is not the doctor, who is it? Who, it may well be wondered, are these stubborn, vindictive gate keepers, these retributivel-minded phantoms? Well, one thing is very clear—they are not phantoms, but real people, pressurized people in positions with little room for manoeu-vre: the Home Office officials. The key thing that Home Office ministers wish to avoid is embarrassing publicity should a patient's recommendation for release be leaked to the media. The case that (although many patients think otherwise) Home Office officials are *not* deliberately awkward, do not willingly try to sabotage patient's chances for it is not the Home Office officials who are to blame, but their situation in a context of being account-able to the vindictive, retributive mass media and general public (who have been indoctrinated by a sensationalized media. The Home Office have to embarrassingly explain themselves, if upon consenting to release of a patient, this is leaked to the popular press and a story plastered all over the front pages. *This* is "political" sensitivity. The Home Office are in a difficult position in wanting to consent to a patient's release at the same time the actual government is strongly advocating a tough law and order policy. The media exploits such an apparent contradiction to devastating effect and casts doubts on the credibility of powers of judgment of the Home Office ministers. After all, it seems very strange for the government to announce tighter measures to affect patients in special hospitals when simultaneously their law department of the Home Office is getting more relaxed in agreeing to more discharges of such patients.

What emerges out of all of this is that of the various parties involved all representing different interests, none of them have unlimited auton-omy—usually because the other interests are always potentially en-croaching upon what little leeway they possess. This is as true for the psychiatrist (who has a reputation to uphold) as it is for the Home Office ministers who have their political standpoints, the credibility of which must not be seen to diminish.

Of course, whilst months of waiting turn into years for the patient due to such political sensitivities, there is a total misconstruing of why this is so. Many people wrongly assume that the reason for a patient doing so long is a clinical one, that no progress has been made—thus a double frustration for the patient. This situation is a sad but also annoying one, when people assume that patients who have spent many years in special hospitals must have done so because they are still very sick and not well enough to be recommended for release by their doctors. The truth is that all of the parties that are involved in the case—be it doctors, nurses, solicitors, Home Office, tribunal panels, and the patients—are irritatingly constrained to act in ways the opposite of what they wish. That is, they are all in agreement that a patient should be released, but due to the media and public opinion cannot effectively engineer many patients' releases in the short term. If they really pushed and stuck their necks out it might stir up such a hornet's nest that their standpoints, even their careers, would be badly damaged.

Hence, another irony. It is not only the patients that are prisoners of a system, without power to decide their release. For even quite senior people, those at the top of the ladder, are themselves tightly hemmed in by a set of uncontrollable constraints. This affects how they will act in the last instance, the decisions that they will consider making, and crucially the ones that will be effectively made.

Summing up, we can appreciate a complex picture of various elements intertwined together, often harmoniously but cut through by an insoluble moral problem of "an eye for an eye" constellation embraced in media reportage and avidly absorbed by the general public. This keeps many a vastly improved patient in a high security hospital quite unnecessarily on clinical grounds. It is here that the matters take on an uneasy, somewhat dubious adherence to professional medical ethics, effectively transcending psychiatry and being a muddy, reputation-upholding scenario.

Perhaps the biggest and most regrettable paradox of is all is that almost everybody wishes to be fair and humane as regards the plight of mentally sick people. Not many people in society are viciously draconian towards the sick, feeling genuinely sorry for them, and are mature and reasonable in the recognition of such a problem as being just one of many in the seemingly unjust, chaotic world in which we find ourselves. Nonetheless, through a complex set of forces many of which in the contexts discussed above are irrational, dilemmas present themselves, seemingly insoluble given such sharply conflicting interests of patients involved. Whether this leads to a conclusion simply of a search for a very elusive sort of future compromise or just disillusionment about human fallibility is not clear.

What is clear, however, is that the problem certainly exists and will not disappear. It could stubbornly take us easily into the next century. Perhaps only a fundamental change in the public conception of mental illness and its connection with crime will resolve the impasse which we are all hopelessly stuck in at present. This is difficult to envisage given the modern media formula for sensationalizing criminality and its relationship to insanity. But it would surely be sad to think that the situation of deprivation of freedom (for those with ample psychiatric excuse for deviant behaviour) would continue, just to ensure the future viability of the modern media.

Such statements do not smack of any revolutionary insightfulness; many of us are aware of preceding problems discussed and, as yet, lack of sound solutions. The whole crux of the problem is seeking to construct a consensus in a society in which so many elements of misperception and potential jeopardization of one's own interests so actively abound. So that it may in the last resort be a situation not so much of human fallibility but of an ultimate desire for protection of self-interest by all people. In turn this gives rise to the strange paradox of us advocating justice for all whilst continuing to maintain a highly individualized self-centredness.

Chapter 8

Getting Better?

Living in society is living on a tightrope. Precariously perched on a wobbliness of what is essentially a continuous construction of social reality, we are the watchdogs of our own survival. Reality is not something we can identify and touch in a reassuring need for substantiation, like a root or a rock upon which we can for all time keep a firm foothold. No. On the contrary, such a need for adherence or security is not guaranteed; we can slip out of such tenuous footholds if we inadequately construct them or, more crucially, fail to reproduce them. If we fail to make events—that is, if we do not forever keep building our routines on an immediate, everyday basis and maintain them—we are a dead species. Only by our actual actions, requiring preconceived thought, can social life persist. But clearly this portrayal of unlimited autonomy in a dreamland of acting on pure whim is both only half the story and not entirely correct either. For we are indubitably constrained. There does and always has existed a definite structuring of our social lives broadly strait-jacketing degrees of leeway we possess.

This is the exact reason for many types of multifaceted differentiation which cuts right across any apparent social, human homogeneity. To believe people possessed social similarities as regards equal access to "goods" and "bads" in society would surely be living in a dream, for as we painfully know, some people are richer, happier, healthier than others; that is, their lifestyles are enormously different. This is not just due to differently possessed physical or mental abilities; certainly biological determinism has some part to play, but can never usurp social factors. It is society which is primarily responsible for a humanity which is essentially heterogeneous. It is a matter of access to the "good" things in life, such as material resources, power, useful contacts. Biology certainly is not the be all and end all of whether you have a good time or not. Of course, in a genetic way we are certainly unique, every one of us, but socially we fall into patterned groups;

the sexually discriminated, the poverty stricken, the career whiz kids, the mentally ill—to cite just a few examples of socially determined clusters of uniformity, of shared circumstances, even though those similar to one another may never even meet.

Such a levelling or patterning effect (of key social denominators) is, in fact, sweeping social, economic, and political forces, worldwide in scope. They implant a definite imprint into the structure of societies through their imposition and long-lived duration in the shape of social institutions. By institutions here we are not referring to hospitals, prisons, or any forcing houses in a narrow everyday terminological sense. For sociologically we are using the concept of institution to embrace all cultural configurations involving human beings—so that institutions are subsets of society—its building bricks containing values, norms, standards, all the ways of behaving by a great diversity of patterned groups. Marriage is an institution, so is a religion, so is the government; in sociological terms institutions are not defunct places, they are living collections of people in similar situations. Such institutions (obviously through mutual membership and familiarity) give rise to an inevitable awareness amongst their members of certain forms of acceptability of ways of behaving. Hence, yardsticks of morality come into being in institutions of which those people that comprise them are informed, behaving usually accordingly.

When we use the phrase "yardsticks of morality," what is implied is a set of conventions about who does what, why they should or shouldn't; equally, what rewards people should have, why some should get more and some should receive less. For people in society are unequally privileged. Some do things which others are not allowed and have rationalizations for this, such legitimation being built into the yardsticks which we implicitly judge, rank, or regard others. It is as if some people are regarded (in value systems) as being qualified (not in an academic sense) to say certain things, perform certain tasks, whereas other people are qualified to do other activities, or allowed to think of certain things, again when other people are not. These different permissible capacities correspond to respective locations in the status hierarchy. People are all (to an extent) judges of others, (although some have more "judging power") in an everyday, almost familiar, unreflecting way. Now, values about what is "good" or "bad," dos and don'ts, may appear purely natural, the only possible or feasible way of going about social life.

73

Yet it could be all very different. For society, or more specifically social reality, can be whatever you want it to be. There potentially exist numerous different realities rather than just the one we are habitually acquainted (and indoctrinated with as unalterable). If previously entrenched structures (here is implied institutions) can be sees as changeable, then their transformation can occur if desired and much hoped-for reforms can materialize. The reason for institutional intransigence, their apparent difficulty in modification or outright replacement, is due to sheer inertia. The legacy of history and its giving to us of an accustomed habituality, coupled with ideological currents in our society, wrongly convince us of institutional inflexibility. For just as the overarching, master variable of social reality can be altered if we so consciously desire, so can its components—the social institutions which make it up. Reality can be restructured, either piecemeal in the shape of moderate reform, or radically revolutionized to clear away obstacles in the way of a more humane, fairer world. Whether this is desired is another matter, but the ability, the capacity for human beings to change their present reality and future destiny is most definitely possible.

Hence, looking at the plight of the less fortunate, they are imprisoned in an oppressive social system due to a legacy of specific historical ideologies. They have been born into an unfavourable social milieux consisting of certain forces unconducive to success for themselves. That is, they have been unable or prevented from flourishing due to their initial location in the social matrix. It is not just material deficiency, but a morality that they clash with. Ideas existing at points in historical time have a structuring effect upon certain groups of people, regardless of such groups abilities; a kind of immaterial determinism. Such groups clash with a prevailing, conventional morality through the reason of having being born into it as losers or undesirables, in not being worthy of the successfulness which others who *are* deemed worthy possess. The mechanism here of differential opportunity allocation and subsequent reward and appraisal is *not* either biologically or materially (financially) derived. Instead, the origin is a peculiar but powerful societal reservoir of philosophies sedimented into it over a long period of time. Some groups get an unequal dose of the stick due to a differential dogma of peculiar moral standards, their evaluation and application.

Even the most powerful of figures in society who possess vast wealth and influence cannot escape this morality—structuring process—that is, their susceptibility of clashing with an incongruent conventionality. We only have to consider King George III to see the progressively diminishing

74

credibility he manifested throughout his biography. At an early stage as almighty ruler, he exacted obedience, love, admiration, respect—he was most truly the King—but at the onset of insanity his influence drastically nosedived; he was no longer qualified to rule, to possess authority, just a sad and sorry lunatic, a joke even. From rule of the kingdom to figure of fun is, to say the least, a staggering status plunge. Quite simply, in tone with the discussion, we see that madness is very tightly excluded from social acceptability; it cannot comfortably be allowed any quarter, in a mainstream societal conventionality of which prides itself on exhibiting only sanity.

Such preceding remarks have perhaps paved the way (set the scene) for our topic of debate now to follow. For we have been talking of moral yardsticks, measures of values, of what is seen as essentially good and respectable, as opposed to some thing seen as atrocious and totally unacceptable. Equally, apart from perceived behaviour, yardsticks help to judge or define an actual personality—good, bad, good leader, a martyr, creative, morbid, useless, mad, whatever. All have in common a socially perceived expression by people of other people's particular psychology; that is, the yardstick is a barometer of which to use upon other people. It measures (correctly or incorrectly) different mentalities. Now it is time to introduce the master yardstick with encompasses all others in social life—the yardstick of *normality*.

Many standards which exist in society all have (at times) a somewhat slippery relativism. They are either unable to exact a total consensus—that is, a commitment by a diverse range of parties—or they do not stand the test of persistence through time. Often it is so that today's "latest," or today's "discovery," will be tomorrow's anachronism. Novelty in both material and mental constructs is perpetually liable to a quality of fleetingness. Perhaps the human mind dislikes the persistence of the familiar but, when offered something new, that too suffers the same fate. So it is with social considerations of that elusive greasy pole we all refer to as *normality*. It is not so much that we strive to approximate too difficult to realize standards, but that quite simply if asked to be precise, probably nobody could exactly state what *normality* is. Even more to the point, even if one party did arrive at what seemed a good definition, others may well refute it as being unacceptable; this implies it is not in *their* sphere of interests to incorporate into *their* lifestyle.

Hence, we can see just why *normality*, grounded as it is in ambivalence, its relativeness, its refusal to be pinned down for actual meaning, renders it totally non-universal as a moral guide. Its implied generality is negated by its incompatible particularism. One of the reasons for this is because we don't know much upon which we can translate thought into definite to-be-followed social rules. And yet the point is that human beings, despite this qualification of rule imprecision, have still gone ahead and actually sought to make rules based upon what they personally conceive to be normality. So that despite being in the dark it was still thought necessary to make often quite hard and fast distinctions between normal and abnormal behaviour. This is in itself at the root of a lot of injustice and perceived injustice in society. More pertinent still, it has had devastating implications for those considered to wander from the normal way of doing things or saying things. And who have been the judges in all of this? Fallible human beings. Themselves. Not only have human beings defined what is normal and what is not, but also who is and who is not.

This has resulted in some people who are mentally unstable wandering free for a lifetime, whilst others, a no more unstable group, being put away, due to power differentials in the capacity to label some more *normal* than others. To be deemed "alright upstairs" is a privilege (due to the possession of power) in a social fluidity of an endless relativity of *normality*.

But this is only the beginning, for if it was simply left just at the above critique of some people assuming themselves to be divine arbiters on the respectability or otherwise of types of morality, it would be disconcerting enough. But now we shall enter some territory that really does open up a Pandora's box. This is the manufacturing of *abnormality* in a system that expressly and proudly proclaims the very essence of a bedrock of unquestionable *normality*.

As the earlier chapters revealed, although societies throughout history have always contained some people on the margins of respectable behaviour, it is nonetheless a distinguishing and peculiar feature of modern society that it has witnessed an increase in mental affliction. So much so that some bodies, not so affected (that is, hitherto never having any connection with such a malaise or its treatment), have become connected insofar as they have begun to ask worrying questions about the rapid upsurge, as has arisen, such as in the U.S.A.

Much more noteworthy is the fact that many people are beginning to question *themselves*, their own mentalities—to try and discern if what they are doing is "all right," if it is straying from some norm or not—*as society defines it.* And it is exactly with the employment of this central, societal gauge (the current conventional wisdom) that the whole process becomes horribly confusing, many people being plunged into self-retrospective chaos. For as we have argued, it has been the actual process which began 200 years ago and is now extremely well set in, that is perhaps the culprit. This dangerously liberating process of loosening our anchorage on a tenuous slippery social reality (living a wobbly existence with others exactly in the same boat). We exist alongside equally worried, concerned minds. It is a moot point, when we consider its legacy, if we have had a net benefit from industrialization considering the mental disorganization left in its wake.

It is clearly a pointless and fruitless exercise to imagine it could be otherwise, or different had it not occurred. But on the other tack it is also a waste of time to contemplate a marked discontinuity or break with the contemporary flow. But that is not to rule out change altogether. We are not blind automatons, hopelessly victimized by impersonal forces. In the final analysis, we construct our reality. Changes can be as easily engineered if so desired by enough people, with enough resources, providing there exists a clear specification of what the problem is, and the political will.

Yet the whole difficulty, as hinted at already, is that despite our knowledge of the problems confronting us, our own individualistic desire for self-preservation in what is definitely a jungle of a remorseless world system renders our voluntaristic entry into a required collectivity (to tackle the problems) almost impossible. Perhaps, as contended in the final chapter, a need not for new leaders as such, but a new politics; that is, different socioeconomic arrangements.

Such preceding digressions help to highlight the connectiveness of seemingly unconnected phenomena. That is, apparently local or isolated problems in society are inter-linked with macro currents of change, particularly the underlying ideologies behind social and economic transformation, as was liberalism with industrialism. Strange as it may seem, such pockets of ideologies enter into how we see, how we evaluate problems which we feel are inherently personal, but they are not personal, or not entirely our own. They are shared throughout society, even though we often think they are not; mental illness being no exception here.

Such an above way of thinking reveals to us that much of modern day mental illness is a direct product of being alive at the present time, of living in society. That is, the price that some people pay for an existence in the modern world is to become prone to, and perhaps succumb to, mental illness, through no fault of their own. But if the trend cannot be entirely reversed it may, as the concluding chapters reveal, be possible to reduce certain elements within such a trend. Here we can look at some of the ways that social and medical science have attempted to put such trend reversal into effect; that is, to counter worldwide socially deleterious patterns which have culminated in such worrying observations as a quarter of North Americans being mentally destabilized.

Whether it be the mildest of tranquilizers or straightforward lobotomy, the entire rationale is the same—to try and treat, rather than "cure." Here we see that even if a "cure" is the intention, it is certainly not a preventative medical approach which is uppermost. Now, just to "cure" is not only a soft option, it is also a fallacy. Has any medical scientist really thought of just what the root cause of the problem to "cure" actually is? Certainly symptoms can be partially checked, but not the continual production of states which cause them to be manifest. It is always shutting the stable door after the horse has bolted.

The source of the entire problem lies within the speed of technical development—its unmitigated, indiscriminate sweep. As complicated as it is, its individual effects upon us cannot easily be pinned down, neither can modern industrialism be criticized as to any of its specific features, which are to be accorded "blame." It is an almost uncontrollable, unidentifiable global set of processes having a momentum of their own. It affects virtually everybody, yet is amazingly unaccountable.

Thus, this is most truly the age of the machine; not necessarily the bad or unwanted machine (for machines are very useful) but rather the rampant, unpredictable machine. It is certainty rather than presence which is largely responsible for our anxieties, our lack of influence to control the machine. One reason is because in our confused enthusiasm we try to solve all problems simultaneously, rather than selectively which might, albeit more slowly, nonetheless produce a more effective outcome. This mistake at trying to cure all things at once is one reason for existing frustrations with existing methods to improve the quality of life of the mentally ill. Only partial success has thereby accrued. Let us delve into this and try and therefore learn from some of the mistakes which have been made.

Often they can be seen wandering around public parks (crying in the rain or standing bewildered amidst hectic shopping precincts), invariably alone. But that's only the visible minority. The majority are clearly "out of sight, out of mind," those who populate our crumbling asylums. Now we confront a very thorny issue—to improve the quality of life. That is a highly vague, sweeping declaration, perhaps smacking of smug condescension, even a wrongful paternalistic patronization. For first of all...what qualities should be instilled? Who has the right to decide? Secondly...what are the supposed undesirable things we wish to remove from patient's minds? Again—who has the right to decide?

Clearly *someone* has had to take the initiative, even if misguided in whatever "treatments" have been dished out over the years. One important aspect of a critique of conventional psychiatric practice is that it has not concentrated upon the most profoundly damaging of "treatments." All too often people have bashed lobotomy, electric shocks, or heavily sedating drugs; fair enough. But the worst kind of treatment, especially concerning long-term side effects, is arguable none of the above kinds of physical or chemical intervention. Such criticisms have narrowly deflected our attention from the equally, if not more significant but more invisible, plight of having been "put away."

This is the process from beginning to end—admission to hospital to discharge (or death whilst still incarcerated)—which is very tough problem to sort out, but if resolved would bring great benefits not just to patients but to medical staff as well and surprisingly to the public. It is, in the long run, a more crucial issue than having continued to focus upon piecemeal projects such as drug or manpower budgets, new forms of nurse training, psychotherapy programmes and such. Certainly such concerns do have some relevance, but tend to be short term, static, almost immediate concerns, which if left to be the only points of focus would just prolong the current impasse. They do not really solve any root causes of difficulties, such as the burden of hospitalization and its subsequent problem of institutionalization (from which all or most of the more micro problems arise).

Having said this, we can also say that many misconceptions abound about what an institutionalized person really is. That is, what they do, what they talk about, how the "come across" having spent a long period inside. The more widely understood (but not most salient meaning) is the notion of a patient having a disproportionate emphasis upon routines which are carried over from the institution upon release into outside life. This is the patient's habitual mental clock. It is a feature which cannot be overlooked. The situation whereby patients who have spent maybe twenty years away encounter severe anxiety upon release if lunch is not exactly at twelve o'clock, or if a cup of tea is not forthcoming at three in the afternoon. This is not really the patient's fault per se—it is due to a hospital monotony of old fashioned, regimented functioning of routines—but is not the really harmful one implied in this context.

The really damaging legacy of an asylum stay is the future scar left to blemish potential future relationships. This is the biggest wound that being shut away for many years can inflict. Being put out of circulation means that, for one thing, there is a huge delimiting down of the range of a whole welter of social encounters—both those consciously entered into plus the potential for interaction of a lifelong basis with a diverse range of people. In society, an adult comes into close contact with different sexes, ages, occupational classes, retail outlets, entertainment organizational personnel, health officials to name but a few comprising a rich, varied, human matrix.

Contrast the above social fluidity with the social life of the hospital inmate. There is the same small group of patients (usually of the same sex and age group), the same ward for years on end, the same doctor, same nursing staff, same psychologist, same social worker, same chaplain. The word "same" is important here as it reveals that not only are there far fewer people in a patient's entire social life (literally society, in fact) but also that those who are present are basically unchanging.

Whereas in mainstream society we meet maybe hundreds of very different people and we might also move our home several times or we may change areas, the patient has none of this human changeability to refreshingly experience. The asylum is the home, full stop. Apart from the occasional newly admitted patient (and notice here a patient), new contact potential is virtually nil. Such interactional limitations and deprivations seriously affect communicational skills, particularly their flexibility (adaptability) to change. Clearly, if you talk to the same group of thirty people for thirty years, then a process is fostered in which dynamic society requiring a dynamic, flexible attitude will not be receptive to a recently discharged patient, who has been away for so long.

Further to this, not only is one who is confined missing out on a lot of newly occurring developments and ideas, both technically and culturally; that is, being prevented from acquiring them. Also, a patient is being rendered less and less capable to adapt to such changes in being unable to learn skills to do so. The overall effect here is not only a "missing out" on a better quality of life for every day one is locked up, but also imprinting a form of depersonalization. Being blunted more and more, socially deskilled more and more, a state of decreased receptiveness to ever, upon release, possessing adequate knowledgeability and social cues to obtain access to what the real world might offer. This is what institutionalization does to people; it denies them a *normal* future. Nothing in much of the more obvious part of the treatment programme can rectify it either; even social skills classes or psychotherapy groups do not sufficiently redress the balance (the harm has done).

Yet that is still not the full cost of damage inflicted. One subtle kind often unknown (unless actually experienced personally) is not just difficulty in handling change, but a set of stultifying effects upon the patient's own self-image. A negative self-esteem can well develop—especially concerning the patient's view of the future. It can tend to be a somewhat short-sighted, unenterprising, unimaginative one, a passive outlook of just "getting through the day," nothing more. Quite literally, taking each day (with its blinkered agenda) as it comes; going right by the book, not only in serious matters, but even in lighter things such as leisure or what little enjoyment is available.

The long-term patient, once released, thus meets a radically changed social and not just material landscape. For society is never a static thing which one can ever rely upon to be at the same spot, same time, every time; it is forever being transformed by its subjects (the human actors) and in turn it modifies them. Society is a malleable entity of webs of relationship, which themselves are perpetually fluid; people age, move jobs, out of areas to new ones, eventually die. People possess an incredible impermanence on a rapidly mobile stage we call society. How then does our discharged patient fare? With a restricted, institutional dialogue, few people to be welcomed by, rusty social as well as occupational skills, little immediate help and guidance seems likely to be forthcoming. Hence it was whilst in the previous existence in society before being put away, the stressful jungle of a society which cracked the person up that caused problem level one—mental disorder. Then problem level two arose from being put away in an institution rendering the patient even less able to cope with society's jungle upon eventual discharge. Problem level three then surfaces: namely, that the society to return to is still a jungle, but now a changed, much unfamiliar jungle, hence a double difficulty of adjustment.

The above comments, far from being a metaphorical exercise, are certainly not abstractions in the real world awaiting newly released patients who have spent many years "inside." Institutionalization is thus not just looking at the clock and expecting one's dinner; it is nothing less than being psychologically crippled in a race with formidable obstacles. The nature of these obstacles awaiting the patient that is, the really fearsome beasts of society's jungle will now be carefully considered.

Chapter 9

Who Cares?

Upon release from hospital, many patients begin a nightmare in what remains the idle dream of the "caring" society. Although the institution they once belonged to had a stultifying, artificial atmosphere, the real world does not necessarily guarantee shelter, adequate food, a bed, or even a few coins in one's pocket. What does exist in order to obtain such meager necessities is a roundabout, convoluted set of procedures of endlessly tiring form filling and wearying walks all over town to agencies to ensure that a claim to a subsistence allowance is legitimate.

The ex-hospital patient is often on a par with the social security scrounger in the eyes of financial personnel sectors of regional health officialdom. Countless case histories meticulously recorded by social workers bear out this fact—if you've nothing on offer, nothing to sell, nothing at all marketable in the closing decades of the twentieth century, then you not only get pushed by the wayside, you remain there.

And remain there discharged patients often do, living in some urban backwater until they can stand the stress, stigma, and shunning no more, going to pieces and remanded back to the institution again where they came from. Usually finance is one of the biggest difficulties. Quite simply, very few members of society are prepared just to give money away; that is, not many benevolent uncles exist. Gifts are a mythology of a distant Dickensian final chapter, not really relevant to now.

Further, if people are without money they cannot afford the prerogative of choice, with choice being anyway a secondary priority subservient to minimal survival. Often some community centre or hostel is the place a recently released patient finishes up in. Here there exists bed and board—that is, a roof over one's head, three meals a day, a few dilapidated items of furniture perhaps, and a television to watch in the main lounge. Not so bad, you might initially think, but wait...who are the *kinds* of fellow lodgers, what are they, where have they come from, what are their circumstances, biographies even?

Invariably, they too have been recently released from mental hospitals, they may not possess adequate finance, and perhaps have a long history of mental problems; they are ex-patients. Now we see a similar sort of process set into operation, similar in many ways to our earlier discussion of the cancerous effects of institutionalization. It is precisely through contact in the same physical setting, be it a hospital or a hostel, with the same limited range of people which can lead to a freeing of social flexibility. For just when a patient (who is already somewhat institutionalized) needs a refreshing contrast of people, after walking out of the hospital gates, the double bind sets in—namely, another smothering of restricted scene and dialogue in the hostel.

It is difficult enough anyway to try and pick oneself up and try and make a fresh start in a world you've been removed from several years, but to go from one place to another—almost exact social blueprints of one another—really does put the lid on it. That is, on one's fate. This is a fate we can now chart, by walking down the same road as a recently discharged patient.

In many ways a return back to square one is the path unwillingly trodden by most upon release. Not only is there a chronic lack of money, but a changed world and changed public, a much altered map of relationships. The social side is most often the stumbling block, but first let us consider the material side of things. In order to get money and enough of it to live above the bare subsistence level, you invariably need to earn it: employment. Now what skills does one possess after asylum style employment? Certainly they are not easily marketable talents (washing up plates, cleaning floors, making beds, wiping walls). Obviously it is unlikely that a change of any professional job will be available (such as accountancy or legal or medical work), for not only would academic qualifications be needed but also a relatively unblemished history—a clean slate. This implies no former criminal record or history of mental disorder.

So, by and large top jobs are most definitely out. What then about more routine employment such as factory or retail work? This may be possible as it does not usually require much specialized knowledge. The only problem here is that there is a lot of competition from people who have the advantage over the patient in possessing a clean legal and medical record.

84

They will most likely therefore be taken on first. So the discharged patient has to keep fruitlessly searching for possibly an ever elusive job.

As hinted at above, part of the difficulty is the artificial kind of work that patients perform in hospital—artificial, that is, when compared with employment in the real world. The term "occupational therapy" is used to describe such activities which often fail to provide a foundation or preparation when released—activities like basket making, painting gnomes, cleaning up piles of leaves in hospital grounds.

This is in no way meant to be a belittling of patients' abilities, however, or the nature of occupational therapy in hospital; for two reasons. Firstly, patients are often a lot more skilled at craft work than non-patients, people out in the community, and patients are also often a lot brighter than people in the community; that is, psychiatric patients are sometimes extremely intelligent people with unusually high IQ levels. Much research confirms this fact. The only hitch is that when they have got the label of ex-patient plus the kind of work they have undertaken whilst in an institution, this does not correspond easily with mainstream occupational opportunities. Equally, patients are not workshy or idle. In a hospital a patient may wash half a dozen staff cars before lunch. The only problem is that there do not exist many jobs in society today of exclusively washing other people's cars all day, by hand, first thing in the morning.

This tails into another important point—the major changes in the economy and corresponding changes in job types. This renders many previously acquired skills (say possessed by patients ten years ago before admission to hospital) redundant. Whilst in hospital the skills in society have become obsolescent, no longer required due to macro processes of technological change. For example, if a patient worked in a quality control department in the mid 1970s, he could well find in the 1990s a lot of computerized operations, little need for human input, fewer human inputs anyway, and perhaps even the actual product made then is no longer made now. In fact, the whole company may have ceased to exist. All of this plus the irremovable stigma associated with having been in a mental hospital makes even manual work very remote.

If a job is not easy to obtain, it could well mean a disillusioning day of rejection after rejection, returning to the familiar office of social security, to claim a sickness benefit and perhaps supplementary benefit. Then back to the hostel to sit in the noisy lounge listening to the incessant chatter and trivia of people in exactly the same situation who have had a very similar day. This may seem to be painting a rather gloomy picture, but the gloom must be darkened a little more concerning the material types of things patients strive for upon release, indeed *must* strive for, if not to flounder and be sent back to hospital.

What, for instance, about learning to drive? This is undoubtedly quite an important asset these days. Well, literally, for most patients this chance is effectively ruled out, if they could not actually afford a car, even a second hand one. But let us just suppose then an ex-patient *could* obtain one, but couldn't drive. Several possibilities arise from this. Firstly, it may quite categorically be written in the patient's medical notes that due to being mentally ill or on medication, driving is not allowed in that case. That is, it is felt that to drive might be a hazard for the patient or other motorists. But say even this limitation did not apply; that the patient did purchase a vehicle, what then? Well, permission to initially take driving lessons may not prove easy but, if granted and a car bought, there are problems of finance to obtain petrol and pay for car maintenance, which might exert a considerable drain on limited resources. Such things as personal transport constitute just one of those increasing necessities (and hence no longer former luxuries) needed to live an adequate existence in society today.

So much for the more obvious material side of problems facing those upon release. What of more subtle but arguably more critical ones? here we are again returned to the area of consistently satisfying and fulfilling relationships. Straightaway in an impersonal world those members of the public that ex-patients come into contact with have a somewhat reserved air. It may even be an attitude of suspicious stigma. The attitude will be primarily founded upon ignorance and worries as to whether the patient is in any way dangerous. The ignorance arises mainly through unfamiliarity with such a type of person, but also often a lack of necessary empathy and tolerance on the public's part.

On the streets, in the shops, at the football match, the party, the disco, the restaurant, the swimming baths, or even on a visit to the dentist, the standoffish distancing, the attitude of disdain often inevitably reveals itself. This being so, it will instill in ex-patients a sense of rejection, being surrounded by hostility, giving the feeling that one is somehow inadequate, even *abnormal*, a misfit upon release into an unwelcoming milieux.

It is not necessarily that patients cannot cope upon release, cannot make it in the real world, but that through a complex combination of circum-stances, their biographies clash all along the line with society which unmovably denies chances or an understanding sympathy. This is why many patients come unstuck, only to get sent back to hospital again; society denying any responsibility in having had a major part to play in this.

Such a low status is reflected in the minimal role patients play (whilst in hospital) in political involvement. Political participation in many custodially minded units is denied—patients in special hospitals are never allowed to vote, for example, and again society has a neat and readily produced rationale of why this should desirably be so. It runs like this: that mental illness is synonymous with a state of irresponsibility, and from that the patient, if allowed to vote, would be making an irrational or illogical choice. Thus a patient's vote is seen as unworthy and meaningless, something best avoided.

And it gets worse. For it might be thought that at least there was some light—such as going home to live with one's family upon release, to be warmly embraced with welcoming arms. Sometimes this works wonderfully, the family having always kept in close touch, but it is for the small minority of patients, those who luckily avoid the hostel or day centre. But still even for those who do go home to relatives, difficulties can set in, usually surfacing after an initially exciting few weeks.

After all, it may well have been a long time away from both the intimate familiarity of one's kin, one's home (it may even be a changed address). Most of all, people will have changed; young brothers now married men; dad dead; baby daughter an independent teenager living away from home; mother largely housebound due to physical infirmity. This situation is summed up in a phrase ex-patients often state upon dismaying exposure to the real world, namely: "It's not the same any more."

This can be extremely harmful to self-esteem which needs to be absolutely positive, but is being eroded for the patient constantly in a very negative, disappointment-after-disappointment sort of way. If you cannot ever really return to a place called home, what can you do? But even if you could "go home," it wouldn't be really a natural experience anyway, for as we have seen, things for patients who have been away a long time have altered so much. "Home," if it still exists, is now just a *place*.

For the person who was married, then sent to hospital, divorce is usually the inexorable outcome, it being impossible to sustain a relationship if separated even partially, for such a bond can only really flourish outside an institution for both partners, not whilst one of them is detained indefinitely within. Such a recognition of this mutually leads to unwanted separation, for institutions are seldom kind to social relationships. They eat at them, can often destroy them. Institutions separate people, divide them, fragment them, replacing one time familiarity with a vacuum.

This vacuum the patient gets more and more absorbed into the institution, becomes part of it, lives it. The remains of one's family outside go in quite different, unexpected directions, living their own lives as the years of incarceration of one of their flesh and blood remorselessly grind on.

Such views are not new; lots of people realize the above plights which hit patients and families, so much so that in recent years we have seen the rise of after-care facilities spring up, know as "community care." Now, wherever the ex-patient is actually living, certain restrictions are imposed. This may be to report for a fortnightly injection of medication or to compulsorily attend a discussion group at a local centre with a psychotherapist. Or if very lucky may receive individual therapy—that is, one-to-one counseling—but this is rare. On such discussions patients can get it "off their chest," "let off some steam," that is, voice their discontent and hopefully get advice from trained therapists, specialists in after-care.

So they discuss their problems, but everybody in the discussion (including the psychotherapist) knows all this already. Simply talking about it week after week will not *solve* such problems. A patient, if given the choice between an immediate lump sum of cash or an idle chat about employment opportunities arising possibly in the future, would take the former option. When you are broke, need money badly, you don't speculate about the future financial situation. It is the here and now, the present, that counts.

Hence, both social and material supports are needed plentifully and consistently; a situation currently not apparent. But looming behind such difficulties are the wider, unstoppable processes we studied in detail earlier, which are generating the whole problem (that of psychiatric disorder) in the first place. This is the way the modern ethos helps to accentuate mental instability in society. This we have contended is virtually impossible to reverse, let alone slow down. Many of us cannot see further than our immediate everyday concerns in a hectic maelstrom of dizzy contemporary living. It's often *having*, not *choosing*, to look after number one.

In the midst of the storm is the mental patient, surrounded by *normal* people who have not as yet succumbed to breakdowns. Yet as suggested earlier, it is a peculiarly new thing that a rapid increase in mental problems is essentially a feature only of late twentieth century existence, a time when many of us have more affluence than ever before. So it seems strange that so many of us should, in fact, be so neurotic, distressed, depressed, whatever. Unfortunately, in the last fifteen years or so, a distinctive ethos has prevailed which only serves to add fuel to this lamentable fire, to further antagonize already existing problems we have highlighted. This is a political philosophy born in the late 1970s of a twist of laissez faire applied to British society and its economy. It has certainly worsened the situation for psychiatric patients, making it more and more austere. So bad, in fact, that patients' futures may not really be worth living; that is, it may well turn out to be a story with a sad ending, a foregone conclusion.

Chapter 10

A Forgone Conclusion

Preceding pages may have portrayed a smug, even rather arrogant, style in which it may have appeared the author was knowledgeable and could foresee all potential solutions. This is certainly not so. On the contrary, the debates are grounded in confusion, disarray, and often resulting disinterest, even indifference. This book does not intend to be a path breaker at all. Sometimes its contents may well appear (to more qualified people who read it) to possess a rather musty, anachronistic air.

Yet the intention was never to actually add or contribute further to the field. Instead, we encountered an in-depth review of existing contributions, with the resultant realization that the last thing that was required would be to try and be a path breaker, to try and increase an already voluminous body of knowledge. This realization was closely connected with a feeling that it is not so much a matter of finding out more about mental disorder, but instead effectively and correctly utilizing the already-existing knowledge we possess and in so doing having to do things we had hitherto neglected— to grasp the nettle of no longer just talking about solutions but to actively implement them. It is an issue of motivational, purposeful intent, not ignorance of the subject matter which is largely responsible for such lethargy and its drag upon developments.

However, you could quite reasonably object to the approach and viewpoints of the contents of this book: a cool, laid back, academically objective analysis, which despite some insightfulness, smacks of being too verbose. But, like it or not, verbosity is the name of the game in mental health discussions, policies, meetings, and research. Such a "word industry" is due to the inherent subjectivity of the topic which requires a flexible style of discourse and perspective. You cannot easily quantify the mind. You cannot measure, let alone see or easily attempt to identify, the content of intensity or feeling of depressions, hallucinations, or paranoia. All you can do is to try and find out, by talking, more about it. But this is the essence: talking to a certain extent, not in a limitless fashion.

For, as said above, the time has come, long overdue, to *use* what we now know to put into motion plans and not rarefied ideas, to seriously try and reduce a growing malaise in modern life; one that will not just go away and, if not addressed, will pose massive problems for populations of the future.

But, of course, it is a much easier option to leave a problem to the future as that nicely prevents effort, time, and money having to be expended now. So often does a future generation have to try and resolve a problem which is far worse than its lackadaisical predecessors encountered, ignored, and bequeathed. But here we cannot assume that it would be soon tackled even if people wished to do so; that is, even if the public and authorities felt so inclined.

This is because there are numerous other serious (some might say more serious) problems demanding solutions in society, deserving more priority. But this is *not* to phrase the debate logically. For it is not simply a superficial list of priorities equally competing with one another. It is a set of different problems represented by interest groups or spokespeople who possess differential amounts of power and hence political clout. Such representation bodies for the mentally ill are quite thin on the ground when it comes to power.

Although small bodies (which are either self-financed or not wealthy at all) such as M.I.N.D. or the National Schizophrenic Association exist, whether they possess much *impact* is another matter entirely. In 1974, a few hundred thousand mine workers effectively brought down the British government, whereas millions of people in British society who are psychiatrically ill cannot conceivably cut such ice. They find difficulty in achieving solidarity (due to the fragmentation within) due to their disability and consequent lack of articulational effectiveness.

So, now we can ask who (if anybody) in society might be prepared to successfully champion the cause of the mentally ill, for enhancing their dignity and improving their life chances, to the awareness of all. A wonderful ideal, yes, but for reasons now to be considered perhaps just that—an ideal.

If not utopian, the task is a staggering one. For after all, what is humane about modern humanity? Two mass genocides this century,

91

greatneglectoftheunderprivileged(disadvantaged),andridiculousechoes from "concerned" leaders of democracy, equal rights, and an end to want. Is it more accurate to see humanity not as humane, but a reckless species greedily and blindly rushing through the centuries of its own self constructed fate? Some steps forward, many steps back.

Is perhaps the only worthy record of what might be called "achievement" to lie in the private sphere of love and possibly a still alive spark of respect for others by so-called "ordinary" people? This being overshadowed by a global roof of greed, destruction, and irresponsibility. And yet, is this particularly surprising? For why should humanity be anything else? Of an otherwise different mentality from the woeful state it currently is or ever was? For better or for worse (and it seems to be for worse), hindsight is the most speculatively useless method of making evaluationaly worthwhile comparisons when used in an idealistic or philosophical way. *This* is what we are is the reality now. That is undeniable, requires no imaginative capacity—just mediocre, unqualified, everyday vision. Can we really (as arrogant philosophers) deny a truth everybody knows, feels, is aware (painfully) of?

Having now brutally introduced realism in the place of idealism, let us set out arguments within the correct framework, namely that of *reality*; or at least the reality for the future of the mentally ill. Restricting (due to great lack and unavailability of comparative data) our study to Britain, we will focus especially since 1979 till the early 1990s, particularly on a strange blend of laissez faire doctrines which are unique in their effects as have been applied by successive post-1979 governments. "Leaner and fitter" is usually implied to mean industrial efficiency—the shaking out of apparently superfluous labour, the closing of inefficient plants, so as to reduce costs and boost productivity.

More subtly, however, "leaner and fitter" can be (and has been) applied to the way human beings have had to live their lives over the last decade or so. Things have been (quite non-monetary things) boiled down to a cost-balance sheet, where questions of cost are absolute. Thus time is money; is it viable for people to live in such a way, could it be achieved more efficiently (that is at less financial cost) to the government, are typical post-1979 considerations beneath the political backcloth of laissez faire philosophy. Above all, will this or that action make a profit.

This is taken a step further in that many people's unavoidable misfortunes are not accepted; being discounted as not fully productive and hence unworthy, such people (like the mentally ill) are thrown on top of the heap which grows daily. If you cannot contribute to productive work and profitably (so due to physical or mental inability), you're not only going to find it difficult to survive, you will confront an attitude of questionability as to whether you should be *allowed* to. You are simply "uneconomic," weeded out in the search for the "leaner and fitter."

Such an overall political ethos, introduced initially to combat inflationary pressures, has thus been extended into many other spheres of our lives. It has deeply permeated the fabric of British society. It has led not only to a differentiation in the ranking of certain firms being efficient or not, but also to human beings. Some are seen as more valuable than others and obtaining in reward greater income, status, and prestige.

How, we might ask, is the above line of thought relevant to our own discussion? In many ways the problem that has arisen can be split into a number of different levels. Firstly, those that have suffered the most directly have been, at the risk of tautology, the victims, the patients themselves. A tightening of the health moneybelt has led not only to the plans for building more hospitals to be scrapped (in favour of "community care") but a ruthless running down of existing facilities. Overall, such financial pruning of "locked wards" (then the other wards), symbolized mental health as an easy target—it didn't (and couldn't) offer much resistance. Where privatisation in manufacturing industry was seen as an exciting venture, indeed of high priority, it being seen as more valuable than continuing to look after people who mentally lacked the capacity to complain.

Coinciding with the actual financial axe and rationalization in the health sphere, was an accompanying moral philosophy which could be seen in retrospect of the damage it inflicted, to be called an immoral philosophy. For it has been assumed since the late seventies that what is really at the root of Britain's economic malaise is a lack of "moral fibre." Many people are said to be workshy, lazy, or bone idle and not to know what a day's hard work is. This view was applied with equal venom to a healthy twenty-year-old unemployed man as to a man aged sixty and chronically schizophrenic, both being considered able and fit for work, and if reluctant to be lacking in moral fibre. Thus it was the opinion that if only (and this just as much applies to the sick) people would graft just that little bit harder, we would lift ourselves out of recession. If they didn't respond to this summons then pressures would (and in fact have been) be brought to bear.

The upshot for patients ousted out of hospitals and into hostels, Salvation Army sheds, or simply onto the streets, has been quite catastrophic. Many have been in such a terrible financial mess that their mental and also physical state has worsened. Some have resorted to theft, some have been mercifully taken on by charity groups, and many are unaccounted for—they seem to have just disappeared. And, of course, the final rub: their demise is simply seen as them having been deficient in that magical ingredient of "moral fibre."

How, does, we might wonder, the health service lack "moral fibre" or finance? This question can partly be answered if we now consider another level that has been adversely affected by over twelve years of relentless and remorseless rationalization. This involves those who have to look after the patients, such as doctors, nurses, psychologists, administrators, occupational therapists, pharmacists, and social workers. Many of such people have quit the posts they formerly held and enjoyed; arguably they would have remained had their own levels of remuneration stayed commensurate with the capacities they held. Where have they gone to, where are they now? It is unlikely you would be able to trace them by looking inside other hospitals in the same regions or even in the United Kingdom itself, for many of them are no longer here. They have gone abroad, to places like the United States. *There* the land of opportunity does seem more of a genuine claim than does Britain.

The level of pay, the facilities to work in, the absence of sudden and unsettling cutbacks in finance, make work in the United States more rewarding, longstandingly attractive, and permanent. This is despite a recession affecting the United States of just as great a severity as is affecting us in Britain. It would seem that the American solution likes not necessarily in advocating more "moral fibre" but rather in a more judicious system of budgeting and an altogether different arrangement of priorities concerning central and regional government expenditure. Perhaps it is a contradiction that leaders in Britain and the United States profess such a close, understanding, "special" relationship, when Britain fails to emulate superior American economic lessons.

Are the British too proud? This may seem an insulting kind of question, but here again, is the British consultant who has emigrated to America in any doubt which system makes the most sense? For we cannot forget that economic and social policies are not simply a collection of words and

94

rhetorically hyped-up speeches at election time; they also have effects, very real ones, upon people's livelihoods.

Moving away now from policies and practices, we can shift our attention to the broader and less obvious processes at work in society which will lead not so much to a depressing future but instead perhaps a sad futility. We shall examine a point hinted at earlier regarding the need for a continuation of the "scapegoating function" for members of the public, as yet not mentally afflicted. Also, the closely related issue of the presentation and dramatization of mental illness and deviance associated with it, as portrayed in the popular mass media.

Although people often vociferously claim that the tabloid newspapers are full of trivia and more akin to comics than what a "proper" newspaper should be, they fail to see popular newspapers' life-saving function, which is due to the concepts of *projection* and *displacement*. For although it may well be true that a tabloid contains little serious or factual reportage per se, this is only a small fraction of its real usefulness for readers. For the bulk of the reading, particularly on deviance, enables people to maintain their highly precarious grip on a wobbly reality. Connected with this dangerous existence is the desperate need to bolster a feeling of being mentally well, and also legally self-righteous. This is, to a large degree, made possible by reading of accounts of insane criminals, beasts who are mad and have transgressed and are now safely behind lock and key. For the person reading such accounts, the actual factual content is, in this context, irrelevant (in fact, a purely factual report would not enable this scapegoating exercise to function nearly so well). It is the *ritual* of it all, the pointing of the finger at certain people who can be singled out as individually insane.

Individual identification and labelling is a crucial mechanism here. For if insanity were seen to be a collective malaise, then society's members would panic into a state of frightened disintegration—no longer assured of their own self opinionated *normality*. Social reality could no longer be unreflectingly, unhesitatingly reproduced on an ongoing basis. This is a very crucial point. It can be applied to a lot of previous arguments, not simply crime and insanity, but the discussion earlier about laissez faire doctrines and moral fibre. It is this: society is a highly tenuous enterprise at the best of times anyway. All that is needed to rock it so that it teeters and kneels over into chaos would be a collective realization that everyone in a sense possesses the same amount of propensity to deviant behaviour and, particularly in recent times, the same vulnerability to the onset of psychiatric breakdown. But such an event is effectively and continuously kept at bay. Why? Well, it is forestalled by falsely allowing people to believe (as in fact many do) that crime is irreducibly and individually motivated and committed act, and also that insanity only applies to *other* individuals.

That is, insanity is not seen (or allowed to be seen and understood) as to what is in fact in the modern era a collective susceptibility to social, economic, and politically unsettling change. The hype about individuals stumbling into bad mental states or breaking laws (as being entirely their own fault and responsibility) helps to let off the hook the collective responsibility. It also allows the general public to remain insulated in their own (so far) unblemished legal and mental cocoons.

Yet even if the above masquerades and myths were exploded, there would still remain a little-altered empathy from the general public towards the mentally ill. For as said earlier, sympathy (which *does* exist to an extent) is very different from actually being in someone else's shoes—which is empathy. For precisely because nobody else can actually *feel* the experience, the sensation, the intensity of being mentally unwell as somebody else is, nobody else knows that it is, in fact, exactly like. It seems *this* particular aspect of a lack of empathy and hence incomplete understanding will continue to frustrate the problem.

But such a host of problems are not static; it is a dynamic situation. As mental illness increases, so will the confusion and somebody will have to eventually act, to do something about it; that is one of the biggest headaches facing modern societies. Of course, piecemeal "solutions" have been tried and adopted, but usually only (as was said earlier) if the group pushing for action can muster enough power to make its case heard. And as we know, usually the mass media are not particularly helpful when it comes to promoting (on a positive note) the need for more resources to be put into the mental health domain; all too often they *oppose* it. The media make a case that the mentally ill should not receive any favourable treatment, certainly not out of the "hard working taxpayers" pockets. For it is made to appear that it is the patient's own fault, and that no easy money should be granted to crazy, often dangerous, irresponsible people who don't deserve any help. At best, just keep them ticking over on the margins of mainstream social life, and hope they continue to remain invisible: "out of sight, out of mind."

Hence, the public require them as vital scapegoats and thereby use them, but don't feel it right to reciprocate any assistance. At a wider level, returning to the real genesis of our problem, only a fool could contemplate putting into reverse the process largely responsible; the technological bulldozer of our much-receding desire for mental stability. So long as there is no sudden severe dislocation of the functioning of modern societies, then the twilight zones of psychiatry can remain neatly under the carpet.

So then, does anybody care? Yes. A lot of people do, but rarely those in pivotal positions of decision making. The multinational corporations, for example, do have great influence on virtually everybody on earth, whereas mental bodies, precisely because they do not affect most of us, can afford to be partially ignored. In fact, much debate in the mental health sphere is way down on the list of world agenda of issues to warrant discussion, let alone action. Part of this difficulty quite simply occurs due to the lack of consensus in divided societies as to what should be done, even what or who is responsible for ill health. Given the current global scene, nothing seems likely to suddenly transform such an impasse; a misunderstood stalemate. So is this the end? A doom-laden message for the mentally ill and all those involved in their cause? No, it is not. If there is a continued widening of some of the insights of preceding chapters—to permeate more and more into public cognizance—trees from acorns can, and will, grow. We do not so much therefore need to keep increasing the knowledge of psychiatry, for enough is already clearly known; it is the political will to actually pour in human and financial resources that is most urgently required.

It is *not* by any means now an exclusively psychiatric matter; it straddles many disciplines. It is, furthermore, recognizing the conflictual rather than (wrongly portrayed) consensual nature of world society. And so long as these antagonisms persist, the preoccupation of issues other than mental health will continue to dominate the minds and policies of modern governments. With everyone getting less and less autonomy, self-centredness also enters the scene, pushing out the scope for a much-needed mutual altruism. It could humorously be said in the present pessimistic context that anyone who was optimistic was clearly unhinged "upstairs."

But optimism plus realism must surely, even despite the hazards and drawbacks, be the title of our agenda. For history reveals itself as having vital turning points—made by pioneering people who stick their necks out, even jeopardize their own positions, in sacrificing their own reputational livelihoods for the common good. The motive does not really matter; it is the motivation that counts.

For as has been contended all along, the world and its reality is socially constructed; hence, if so desired is perfectly amenable to efforts at reconstruction. In consciously realizing this many (supposedly) blind, unalterable problems can be solved, all are invitingly open to the human capacity for intervention. This applies as much to technical as it does to religious, economic, cultural, or mental health matters. Solutions *do* exist. They are waiting to be applied both to those at the present moment who are mentally ill and those people who will become so in the future. Public, media, and many countless others involved need to spend some time dispelling negative mythologies of madness and substitute in their place a realistic, understanding appraisal of the terrible tragedy in their midst. They must crucially reach consensus and *do* something positive to reverse a rapidly worsening trend. The psychiatric patients of tomorrow could be the readers of this very book—you or me—nobody is exempt from falling into the net. If things get worse and more unbearable with nobody having attempted to make an effort towards change for the better, then human beings have only got themselves to blame.